FEMALE POETS
OF THE
FIRST WORLD WAR

VOLUME 1

A Centenary Collection
Compiled By Lucy London

Interesting Books...
...Fascinating Subjects!

POSH UP NORTH
Publishing
www.poshupnorth.com

First published in Great Britain in July 2013 by
Posh Up North Publishing
4 Watson Road, Blackpool FY4 1EG

This edition © 2013

Compiled by Lucy London
Edited by Paul Breeze

British Library cataloguing in publication data.
A catalogue record for this book is available from the British Library

ISBN 978-1-909643-02-04 (Print)
978-1-909643-09-3 Kindle Version

"Amid the dust of bookshops, wide dispersed
And never purchased there by anyone
Yet similar to precious wines, my verse can wait
Its time will come..."

Marina Tsvetaeva (1892-1941, Russian – see Volume 2)

This book is dedicated to all those whose lives were lost or altered due to a conflict anywhere on our planet and to those left to learn how to deal with the consequences of war.

In Memory of Kenneth Yule Jackson, Audrey Jackson van der Merwe, Gladys Jean Jackson, James Yule, William Gill Yule Jnr, Robert Rickards (a stretcher bearer in WW1) and Brenda Patricia Rickards (WRAF WW2).

For David, Jimmy and Paul

Note On Content:

Please note that the poets who are included in this book are not necessarily "war poets" as such and, in order to qualify for inclusion in this research project, they only need to have been alive and actively writing during the period of the Great War.

As such, many of the poems that I am citing are not about the war at all, merely written then and some of the poems were not necessarily written during the war at all but beforehand or afterwards.

CONTENTS

INTRODUCTION

We hear much about the 'Western Front' but the First World War covered a vast area - the theatre of war extended across to Russia, down through the Ottoman Empire into Arabia and spilled over into Africa. Other countries of the world were also involved and many sent help to the Allies or to Germany.

World War One was different to anything that had been experienced on battlefields until then. Strangely, roles were reversed – in the trenches womanly caring and nurturing values were needed because dry socks and hot food were vital to keep the soldiers healthy where mud, rats and lice were a constant problem. The women left behind needed to fill the shoes of the men away at war, shouldering tasks and responsibilities they were not brought up to undertake. Apart from keeping the home fires burning, women worked in munitions factories, as bus drivers and conductresses, clerks, secretaries, nurses and on the land - leaving home, travelling far from their families and living away from home – unheard of on such a scale until then.

Women joined the armed forces and served at the Front as nurses and ambulance drivers.   Yet women were not granted the right to vote in the UK until 1928, although the Married Women's Property Act, which meant that a woman's property and children no longer belonged exclusively to her husband upon marriage (with the possibility of losing everything if her husband chose to divorce her) came into force in 1882.

There were many exceptional women – Edith Cavell, a clergyman's daughter from Norfolk was working as a nurse in Brussels when war broke out and was executed in 1915 for helping British soldiers escape after the Battle of Mons. Flora Sandes, a clergyman's daughter from Suffolk, went to the Eastern Front and joined the Serbian Army where she fought until she was wounded.

Elsie Knocker and Mairi Gooden-Chisholm, both keen motorcyclists, went to London as soon as War was declared to join the Women's Emergency Corps and were recruited by Dr. Hector Monro for his Flying Ambulance Corps.

The poet May Sinclair, who was born in Rock Ferry on the Wirral Peninsula, was also a member of the first group of nurses, doctors, orderlies and helpers who went with Dr. Monro and his Corps to Belgium in September 1914.

Dr Elsie Inglis from Edinburgh helped found The Scottish Women's Hospitals for Foreign Service and went to Serbia to treat the wounded, training medical teams that served in all theatres of war.

The war affected everyone in many ways and not just humans either – horses were needed to pull gun carriages and carts and to transport men and machinery to the Front. Those horses had previously been kept as pets or to hunt, work in fields or pull carts, carriages and coaches. They, together with dogs, cats and pigeons played their part in the War to end all Wars that changed society for ever.

Many people wrote about their experiences - some put their feelings into poetry. The soldier poets of the time, such as Wilfred Owen are well-documented. This book will tell you about some of the women who wrote poems during World War One. Many anthologies seem to concentrate exclusively on English-language poets which I feel is a shame. I am currently researching in the hopes that I will find at least one example of a woman who wrote poetry during the 1914 – 1918 period from every country involved in the Conflict.

Researching this subject is very much a 'labour of love', which I really do enjoy. It takes a great deal of time but every day brings a fresh revelation. I have included a list of the poets I have found so far in this volume as it is the first in a series of anthologies which, hopefully, will include a picture, brief biographical details and samples of the work of all the poets I discover.

If you know of a poet or indeed a country, that I have so far not included, please contact me and I will do my best to bring details to the public's attention.

Lucy London,
July 2013

PART ONE: GREAT BRITAIN

*"Britannia" designed by Henry Gates in 1898 as part of "Canada: Patriotics – The Wilson Series" for the
JC Wilson & Company postcard manufacturers in Montreal, Canada.
More information can be found at www.jcwilson.ca*

STELLA BENSON

Born 6th January 1892, Wenlock Edby, Shropshire

Died 6th December 1933, Hongay, Vietnam

Feminist, travel writer, poet, novelist. Friend of Winifred Holtby and Vera Brittain.

Stella was born in Lutwyche Hall, Wenlock Edby (near Easthope) in Shropshire to Rolf Beaumont Benson and Caroline Essex Cholmondeley. Stella's Mother's sister was Mary Cholmondeley, the novelist.

The family were rich and were based in London but travelled a great deal, spending time in Germany and Switzerland. Stella began to keep a diary at the age of ten and continued for the rest of her life. She wrote poetry as well and at the age of thirteen had a poem published in *St. Nicholas* Magazine, New York. Her first volume of poems "Twenty" was published in 1918.

Stella's novels "I Pose" and "This is the End", were published in 1915 and 1917 respectively, followed by "Living Alone" in 1919.

During the First World War, Stella did voluntary work as a gardener and at the Charity Organisation Society in the East End of London. In 1918, she travelled to America where she worked for a time in California before going to China. In China she met her future husband, James O'Gorman Anderson, an Officer in the Chinese Maritime Customs Service. They were married in 1921, honeymooning by driving across America in a Ford car. They travelled extensively for the rest of their lives together.

Stella died of pneumonia in 1933 in Hongay in Vietnam.

Christmas, 1917

A key no thief can steal, no time can rust;
A faery door, adventurous and golden;
A palace, perfect to our eyes--Ah must
Our eyes be holden?

Has the past died before this present sin?
Has this most cruel age already stonèd
To martyrdom that magic Day, within
Those halls, enthronèd?

No. Through the dancing of the young spring rain,
Through the faint summer, and the autumn's burning,
Our still immortal Day has heard again
Our steps returning.

Song

If I have dared to surrender some imitation of splendour,
Something I knew that was tender, something I loved that
was brave,
If in my singing I showed songs that I heard on my road,
Were they not debts that I owed, rather than gifts that I
gave?

If certain hours on their climb up the long ladder of time
Turned my confusion to rhyme, drove me to dare an attempt,
If by fair chance I might seem sometimes abreast of my
theme,
Was I translating a dream? Was it a dream that you dreamt?

High and miraculous skies bless and astonish my eyes;
All my dead secrets arise, all my dead stories come true.
Here is the Gate to the Sea. Once you unlocked it for me;
Now, since you gave me the key, shall I unlock it for you?

Both poems previously published in "Twenty" by Stella Benson
(London: Macmillan, 1918)

AGATHA CHRISTIE

Born 15th September 1890,
Torquay, Devon

Died 12th January 1976,
Wallingford, Oxfordshire

Agatha Mary Clarissa Miller was born on 15th September 1890 in Torquay, Devon. She was the daughter of Clara (nee Boehmer) and Nathaniel Frary Miller, an American stockbroker.

Educated at home, young Agatha's main inspirations were Edith Nesbit, Edward Lear and Lewis Carroll. Agatha's father died when she was eleven years old and after a period at school in Torquay, she was sent to finish her education in France. When she returned to England in 1910, her Mother was ill so they decided to travel to Egypt. By then Agatha was writing novels, poems and music and taking part in amateur theatrical productions.

Agatha met Archibald "Archie" Christie (1889 – 1962) at a dance in Devon in 1912. Archie was born in India, had joined the RAF and was stationed in Devon. They fell in love and became engaged. When World War One broke out, Archie was sent to France and Agatha joined the Voluntary Aid Detachment. The couple were married during Archie's leave in December 1914.

Agatha served with the VAD in Torquay, working in a hospital until the end of the war. Archie was posted to England in September 1918 and they settled in London. They had one daughter – Rosalind who was born in August 1919. They divorced in 1928. Agatha married archaeologist Max Mallowan, who she met in Baghdad.

Agatha Christie went on to become one of the most famous and best-loved authors in the world and was awarded a CBE in 1956 and the title of Dame in 1971.

She died on 16th January 1976.

World Hymn 1914

Thunder of guns and clash of steel!
Fashion it out with lathe and with wheel.
These are the masters of men today;
Men who created, and men who pay.
A hum in the sky
Where the war birds fly,
Battle, murder, and sudden death,
Women who pray with a catch in their breath,
The God of War is nigh!

Thunder of guns, and clash of steel!
Women who work, and women who kneel,
Crying aloud: "How long, how long?
Before the right shall defeat the wrong?"
Silence and Peace
Rest and Release!
Hearts that are fainting beneath the strain
Call upon Heaven in passionate pain,
Call to the God of Peace.

Thunder of guns, and clash of steel!
All the way through, for woe or for weal,
The throb of a People's heart that is breaking,
The stir of a People's soul that is waking . . .
And beneath the roar
Of the weapons of war,
A Silence set in the midst of Sound. . .
And a Voice that shall never again be drowned . . .
The Unknown God is speaking . . .

Easter 1918

Let us today know only great rejoicing,
Nor mourn our gallant dead, so young and gay
Like Easter flowers
That stand in youthful vigour straight and golden,
Those Easter flowers which fill the world today!
Let now be ours
The wider vision (though our eyes be holden)
The deeper understanding that shall see
Death as a change which comes at Life's beginning,
A joyous rushing of young souls set free. . .

Let us not mar the splendour of their going!
Their loving and their laughter shall not cease.
So shall we almost hear, for ever growing
Out of the silent darkness day by day,
The rushing sound of a triumphant massing!
Oh! Let us then acclaim that valiant passing
Which some call Death – and others name Release!

Both poems were first published in "The Road of Dreams" by Agatha Christie Mallowan. (London: Geoffrey Bles, 1924)

WINIFRED HOLTBY

Born 23rd June 1898,
Rudston, Yorkshire

Died 29th September 1935

Winifred was born in Rudston, Yorkshire. Her Father was David Holtby and her Mother, Alice, was the first woman to be an Alderwoman on the East Riding County Council. Winifred went to St. Margaret's School in Scarborough and was going to go to Oxford in 1917 but instead joined the Women's Army Auxiliary Corps and in early 1918 she was sent to France as part of a signals unit.

In 1919, Winifred went up to Oxford, where she met Vera Brittain who became her life-long friend and in 1921 she became one of the first women to be awarded a degree by that University.

Winifred was a feminist, pacifist, writer, poet and journalist – working for The Manchester Guardian, Daily Express, Evening Standard, Good Housekeeping and The News Chronicle. Winifred's debut novel "Anderby Wold" was published in 1923.

She travelled widely, lecturing for the League of Nations, wrote a book about Virginia Woolf, which was published in 1932 and "Women in a Changing Civilisation" for the Women's Movement, which was published in 1934.

In 1931, she was diagnosed with Brights Disease and she died in 1935.

Of all the 14 books Winifred wrote, the most famous – the novel, "South Riding", which was published in 1936 after her death - was made into a film and twice into a television series. Hull History Centre holds many of Winifred's papers and an academy school in Hull has been named after her.

Trains In France

All through the night among the unseen hills
The trains,
The fire-eyed trains,
Call to each other their wild seeking cry,
And I,
Who thought I had forgotten all the War,
Remember how a night in Camiers,
When, through the darkness, as I wakeful lay,
I heard the trains,
The savage, shrieking trains,
Call to each other their fierce hunting-cry,
Ruthless, inevitable, as the beasts
After their prey.
Made for this end by their creators, they,
Whose business was to capture and devour
Flesh of our flesh, bone of our very bone,
Hour after hour,
Angry and impotent I lay alone
Hearing them hunt you down, my dear, and you,
Hearing them carry you away to die,
Trying to warn you of the beasts, the beasts !
Then, no, thought I ;
So foul a dream as this cannot be true,
And calmed myself, hearing their cry no more.
Till, from the silence, broke a trembling roar,
And I heard, far away,
The growling thunder of their joyless feasts –
The beasts had got you then, the beasts, the beasts –
And knew
The nightmare true.

First published in "Time and Tide", 1931

*A train journey in France after the War, brought back memories of Winifred's time on
The Western Front in 1918*

The Saraband – A Coward's Apology – 1920

So you are angry, will not take my hand,
Nor laugh to me again with loving eyes ;
But lift your charming head with hurt surprise
Half scornful. Dear, you do not understand,
Down music-haunted halls we bow and sway,
Moving in measured figures, gravely planned ;
Not knowing what wild air the minstrels play.
You hid your anger with disdainful face
Thinking 'twas I who gave the sidelong glance,
Tortured your soul upon a turn of chance.
Because I trod my measure out of place
You thought I wittingly forwent your grace,
It was not I, dear heart. It was the Dance.

The Harvest Fields Of Fair Lorraine

The harvest fields of fair Lorraine
Were crowned with yellow corn,
And midst the gold were crimson heads
By poppy stems up borne.
In dewy morn the peasants reap,
In quivering heat of noon,
Till o'er the purple hill-top glides
The primrose harvest moon.
The harvest fields of fair Lorraine
Are not so gold as then,
And midst the gold are crimson stains,
The blood of fallen men;
And by the light of one lone star
And the chill wind's sobbing breath,
A reaper gathers his harvest there -
And the reaper's name is Death.

Previously published in "Testament Of Friendship: The Story Of Winifred Holtby" by Vera Brittain, (London: Macmillan, 1940)

WINIFRED MABEL LETTS

Born 10th February 1882
Salford, Lancashire

Died 7th June 1972
Dun Laoghaire, Ireland

Winifred was born on 10th February 1882 in Broughton, Salford, County of Lancaster (now Greater Manchester). Her father was English – a member of the Letts Diaries family – and her mother Irish. After her father's death, Winifred and her Mother moved to Ireland. Winifred went to school at Abbots Bromley and then to college in Dublin.

Winifred's career as a writer began in 1907 when she had her first two novels published – "Waste Castle" and "The Story Spinner" - as well as having a one act play perfomed at the Abbey Theatre in Dublin. In 1913 she published her first collection of poetry called "Songs From Leinster" - some of which were set to music by C.V. Standford, the most famous being "A Soft Day".

During the First World War, Winifred joined the Volunteer Aid Detachment as a nurse at Manchester Base Hospital and then trained as a masseuse with the Almeric Paget Military massage Corps and worked at army camps in Manchester and Alnwick, Northumberland.

In 1916, she published a book of poems called "Hallowe'en and Other Poems of the War". This volume of poems was so popular that it was re-printed in 1917 and renamed "The Spires of Oxford, and other Poems".

In 1926, Winifred married a widower - William Henry Foster Verschoyle. He was 67 and had lost 2 of his 3 sons in the Great War.

Winifred continued to write and had numerous works published throughout the 1930s, most notably "Knockmaroon" – published in 1933 – which was a volume of memoirs where she wrote about her childhood holidays spent at her mother's family home at Phoenix Park in Dublin. This contained illustrations by her stepdaughter Kathleen Verschoyle.

After her husband's death, Winifred lived for a time in Faversham, Kent with her sisters Dorothea Williams and Mary Letts but she moved back to Ireland in the early 1950s and lived at Beech Cottage in Killiney, County Dublin for many years.

She died on 7th June 1972 at the Tivoli Nursing Home in Dun Laoghaire and is buried in Rathcoole, County Dublin.

She leaves a legacy of plays, novels, books, poems and songs.

Bairbre O'Hogan knew Winifred Letts personally as she had been a friend of Bairbre's mother for over 40 years. Bairbre fondly recalls, as a young girl, accompanying her on occasional shopping trips and stopping off at cafes in Dun Laoghaire and visiting her home and wonderful garden where Winifred could roll off the common and botanical names of all the plants.

The portait photo of Winifred shown on the previous page comes from Bairbre's mother's own first edition copy of "Knockmaroon" which Winifred gave her – suitably inscribed – and into which she physically stuck that photograph of herself.

The photo on this page is a personal photo taken while out on a picnic wth Bairbre's family around 1968.

Bairbre is researching WM Letts' life and works and was kind enough to allow us to use some of her notes for this brief biography.

She is happy to hear from anyone with queries or information about WM Letts by email to: researchingwmletts@gmail.com

17

Spires Of Oxford

I saw the spires of Oxford
As I was passing by,
The gray spires of Oxford
Against the pearl-grey sky.
My heart was with the Oxford men
Who went abroad to die.

The years go fast in Oxford,
The golden years and gay,
The hoary Colleges look down
On careless boys at play.
But when the bugles sounded war
They put their games away.

They left the peaceful river,
The cricket-field, the quad,
The shaven lawns of Oxford,
To seek a bloody sod—
They gave their merry youth away
For country and for God.

God rest you, happy gentlemen,
Who laid your good lives down,
Who took the khaki and the gun
Instead of cap and gown.
God bring you to a fairer place
Than even Oxford town.

Previously published in "A Treasury of War Poetry – British And American poems of the world war 1914-17", edited by George Herbert Clarke. (Boston, USA: Houghton Mifflin, 1917).

The Deserter

There was a man, - don't mind his name,
Whom Fear had dogged by night and day.
He could not face the German guns
And so he turned and ran away.
Just that - he turned and ran away,
But who can judge him, you or I ?
God makes a man of flesh and blood
Who yearns to live and not to die.
And this man when he feared to die
Was scared as any frightened child,
His knees were shaking under him,
His breath came fast, his eyes were wild.
I've seen a hare with eyes as wild,
With throbbing heart and sobbing breath.
But oh ! it shames one's soul to see
A man in abject fear of death,
But fear had gripped him, so had death;
His number had gone up that day,
They might not heed his frightened eyes,
They shot him when the dawn was grey.
Blindfolded, when the dawn was grey,
He stood there in a place apart,
The shots rang out and down he fell,
An English bullet in his heart.
An English bullet in his heart !
But here's the irony of life, -
His mother thinks he fought and fell
A hero, foremost in the strife.
So she goes proudly; to the strife
Her best, her hero son she gave.
O well for her she does not know
He lies in a deserter's grave.

Previously published in "Hallow-een And Poems Of The War", by WM Letts.
(New York: EP Dutton & Company, 1916).

MARGARET ROWNTREE

Born 1899, Fleetwood, Lancashire

Died 13th February 1983, Fleetwood, Lancashire

Photo kindly supplied by Gladys Smith of Fleetwood, Lancashire

Margaret E Fish – nicknamed Lily - was born in Fleetwood. Both her grandfathers were Master Mariners and her Father was a Trinity House Pilot and went on to be Fleetwood's Deputy Harbourmaster. Her grandfather WA Simpson was an Alderman of the Borough of Fleetwood and went on to Mayor in the 1930s.

Margaret attended Chaucer School and Blackpool Grammar School and then went on to train as a teacher at Edge Hill College in Liverpool.

Margaret became a teacher, teaching first at her old school – Chaucer - and then after the death of her husband, Lawrence Rowntree, in 1947 she taught at Tyldesley School, Blackpool.

She was a keen writer of poems and prose throughout her life with her earliest works being published in the Blackpool Grammar School magazine. In later years, many of Margaret's poems were published in "Lancashire Life" magazine and in the local press and in 1977 she poduced a collection of her best work called: "Sixty Years Of Verse".

In later life, Margaret Rowntree went on to be a town councillor and the first lady mayor of the Borough of Fleetwood and was awarded an MBE. She died in 1983 but her name lives on in the form of the Margaret Rowntree Trophy which is presented every year at the Fleetwood Music & Arts Festival

Keep Faith

Keep faith with us, the men who died
To save a people's soul from shame
Across the country, far and wide,
Our poppies blaze a trail of flame,
Red as the blood we shed for you
In lands across an alien foam
That you may keep a nation's due
To live in freedom here at home.

Keep faith with us, the common men
Who left the ways our fathers trod
Took up the sword and walked again
Where men were face to face with God.
His holy aid helped us to die
O you that follow ask that aid
That you may keep the liberty
That makes a people unafraid.

Keep faith, we ask no other price
We fought that wars should have an end
There is no greater sacrifice
Than that a man die for his friend.
You were our friends, we died for you
Live then to glorify our death
That a bewildered world may know
The peace that dwelt at Nazareth.

Margaret Fish

*Originally published in "Virginibus Pueresque" The Blackpool Grammar School
Magazine in 1916*

Any Widow In Any War

Low lies the lad who lay with me,
Him I loved in the warm, dark night,
Dead and cold is his ecstasy
And fled forever our dear delight.

I am alive or so it seems,
Yet from me death can nothing take
For he is dead, save in my dreams,
And I die daily when I wake.

All that we loved is lovely still
Yet it can never be the same.
O you that shape the peoples' will
Think how you best may bear the blame.

And all you millions who like me
Loss such as mine alike must share,
Own the responsibility
Know that we too the blame must bear,

Leaders and led have missed the call
That could have brought us to the light.
'Tis for the folly of us all
That I lie lonely through the night.

Oh! let the bloody battles cease,
People to people hear my plea,
Build for yourselves the endless peace
That none can ever bring to me.

Margaret Fish

*Originally published in "Virginibus Pueresque" The Blackpool Grammar School
Magazine in 1916*

FREDEGOND SHOVE

Born 1889, Cambridge

Died 9th September 1949
Cambridge, UK

Photo: Fredegond Shove ca 1925
by Lady Ottoline Morrell

Fredegond was born Fredegond Cecily Maitland to Frederic William Maitland, a historian, and his wife Florence Henrietta nee Fisher. Fredegond was a niece of the first wife of Ralph Vaughn Williams. After her father's death, Fredegond's mother married Francis Darwin, son of Charles Darwin.

Fredegond married Gerald Shove, an economist. Gerald was a conscientious objector and during the First World War they lived and worked on a farm. She continued writing poetry until her death.

Some of Fredegond's poems were chosen by Sir Edward Marsh for the 1918 – 1919 volume of his "Georgian Poetry" series. The only other woman poet to be included in Sir Edward's anthologies was Vita Sackville-West in the 1920 – 1922 volume.

Vaughan William set some of her poems to music in 1922 under the title "Four Poems by Fredegond Shove" for baritone voice and piano.

After Fredegond's death in 1949, her sister Ermengard had a small book about her sister and brother-in-law privately printed – "Fredegond and Gerald Shove". In 1956 a small anthology of Fredegond's verses was published by Cambridge University Press.

The Farmer, 1917.

I SEE a farmer walking by himself
In the ploughed field, returning like the day
To his dark nest. The plovers circle round
In the grey sky; the blackbird calls the thrush
Still sings but all the rest have gone to sleep.
I see the farmer coming up the field,
Where the new corn is sown, but not yet sprung;
He seems to be the only man alive
And thinking through the twilight of this world.
I know that there is war behind those hills,
And I surmise, but cannot see the dead,
And cannot see the living in their midst
So awfully and madly knit with death.
I cannot feel, but know that there is war.
And has been now for three eternal years.
Behind the subtle cinctures of those hills.
I see the farmer coming up the field,
And as I look, imagination lifts
The sullen veil of alternating cloud,
And I am stunned by what I see behind
His solemn and uncompromising form:
Wide hosts of men who once could walk like him
In freedom, quite alone with night and day,
Uncounted shapes of living flesh and bone,
Worn dull, quenched dry, gone blind and sick, with war;
And they are him and he is one with them;
They see him as he travels up the field.
O God, how lonely freedom seems to-day!
O single farmer walking through the world,
They bless the seed in you that earth shall reap,
When they, their countless lives, and all their thoughts,
Lie scattered by the storm: when peace shall come
With stillness, and long shivers, after death.

First published in "Dreams And Journeys" by Fredegond Shove
(Oxford: BH Blackwell, 1918)

MAY SINCLAIR
(Mary Amelia ST. CLAIR)

*Born 24th August 1863
in Rock Ferry, Wirral, UK*

*Died 14th November 1946
In Bierton, Buckinghamshire*

Mary Amelia St Clair was the youngest of the six children - only daughter - of a wealthy Liverpool shipowner – William Sinclair. May's father went bankrupt and died when May was in her teens. May and her family then moved to Ilford, near London. She attended Cheltenham Ladies College for a year before returning home to look after her brothers – four of whom died early deaths from heart defects.

In 1886, she published her first volume of poetry – "Nakiketas and Other Poems" - under the name Julian Sinclair but when she had to start earning a living from writing in order to support herself and her ailing mother, she adopted the penname for which she is best known - May Sinclair.

May was already a successful author well before the First World War period, having published numerous novels and collections of stories, as well as a highly respected biography of the Brontë Sisters called "The Three Brontës".

She was a keen supporter of the Suffragette movement and wrote pamphlets for the Woman Writers Suffrage League

When World War One broke out, May joined Dr. Monro's Flying Ambulance and went to Belgium in September 1914. By then she was 52, which in those days, was 'old'.

Shortly afterwards, May returned to England suffering from shell shock and wrote about her experiences in *A Journal of Impressions in Belgium*, published in New York by Macmillan in 1915.

Three of May's nephews enlisted – two died and one spent much of the War as a prisoner of war and returned home ill with pneumonia. May nursed him back to health.

Sinclair was one of the early Modernists and, as well as her novels and literary critiques, also wrote non fiction on subjects varying from Imagism, Freudian psychology and German philosophical idealism.

In April 1918, May Sinclair was the first to use the term originally invented by psychologist William James "stream of consciousness" – or interior monologue – as a literary technique to describe Dorothy Richardson' s narration in the book "Pilgrimage" in a review that she was writing for "The Egoist" journal.

She was a prolific writer from the 1880s through until the late 1920s when she was diagnosed with Parkinson's disease and decided to give up writing. She retired to live in Buckinghamshire and died in 1946.

Dedication (To a Field Ambulance in Flanders)

I do not call you comrades,
You,
Who did what I only dreamed.
Though you have taken my dream,
And dressed yourselves in its beauty and its glory,
Your faces are turned aside as you pass by.
I am nothing to you,
For I have done no more than dream.

Your faces are like the face of her whom you follow,
Danger,
The Beloved who looks backward as she runs, calling to her lovers,
The Huntress who flies before her quarry, trailing her lure.
She called to me from her battle-places,

She flung before me the curved lightning of her shells for a
lure;
And when I came within sight of her,
She turned aside,
And hid her face from me.

But you she loved;
You she touched with her hand;
For you the white flames of her feet stayed in their running;
She kept you with her in her fields of Flanders,
Where you go,
Gathering your wounded from among her dead.
Grey night falls on your going and black night on your
returning.
You go
Under the thunder of the guns, the shrapnel's rain and the
curved
lightning of the shells,
And where the high towers are broken,
And houses crack like the staves of a thin crate filled with
fire;
Into the mixing smoke and dust of roof and walls torn
asunder
You go;
And only my dream follows you.
That is why I do not speak of you,
Calling you by your names.
Your names are strung with the names of ruined and
immortal cities,
Termonde and Antwerp, Dixmude and Ypres and Furnes,
Like jewels on one chain--
Thus,
In the high places of Heaven,
They shall tell all your names.

MAY SINCLAIR. March 8th, 1915.

First published in "A Journal of Impressions in Belgium" by May Sincair.
(New York: Macmillan, 1915)

Field Ambulance In Retreat
Via Dolorosa, Via Sacra

A straight flagged road, laid on the rough earth,
A causeway of stone from beautiful city to city,
Between the tall trees, the slender, delicate trees,
Through the flat green land, by plots of flowers, by black canals thick
with heat.

The road-makers made it well
Of fine stone, strong for the feet of the oxen and of the great Flemish
horses,
And for the high wagons piled with corn from the harvest.
And the laborers are few;
They and their quiet oxen stand aside and wait
By the long road loud with the passing of the guns, the rush of
armored cars and the tramp of an army on the march forward to
battle;
And, where the piled corn-wagons went, our dripping Ambulance
carries home
Its red and white harvest from the fields.

The straight flagged road breaks into dust, into a thin white cloud,
About the feet of a regiment driven back league by league,
Rifles at trail, and standards wrapped in black funeral cloths.
Unhasting, proud in retreat,
They smile as the Red Cross Ambulance rushes by.
(You know nothing of beauty and of desolation who have not seen
That smile of an army in retreat.)
They go: and our shining, beckoning danger goes with them,
And our joy in the harvests that we gathered in at nightfall in the
fields;
And like an unloved hand laid on a beating heart
Our safety weighs us down.
Safety hard and strange; stranger and yet more hard
As, league after dying league, the beautiful, desolate Land
Falls back from the intolerable speed of an Ambulance in retreat
On the sacred, dolorous Way.

First published in "A Journal of Impressions in Belgium" by May Sinclair.
(New York: Macmillan, 1915)

EDITH SITWELL

*Born 7th September 1887,
Scarborough, Yorkshire*

*Died 9th December 1964
London*

Edith Sitwell portrait by Roger Fry 1915

Edith Louisa Sitwell was born on 7th September 1887 in Scarborough, North Yorkshire. She was the eldest child and only daughter of Sir George Sitwell, the Fourth Baronet of Renishaw Hall, who specialized in genealogy and landscape gardening.

Edith had two brothers – Osbert (1892 – 1969) and Sacheverell (1897 – 1988) who would later join her in forming a significant modernist literary circle.

After a rather tempestuous childhood, Edith moved into a small flat in Bayswater which she shared with Helen Rootham who had been her governess since 1903. Her first poem, entitled "The Drowned Suns" was published in The Daily Mirror in 1913 and she followed this in 1915 with her first collection - "The Mother and Other Poems" published by Blackwell.

Between 1916 and 1921 the Sitwells edited an annual collection of poems under the title "Wheels" and Edith became a supporter of new trends in English poetry. Her flat became a 'salon' where young poets met and WB Yeats, TS Eliot, Virginia Woolf, Robert Graves and Aldous Huxley were all regular visitors.

She took great interest in the war and met soldier poets Siegfried Sassoon and Wilfred Owen and, after his death, Edith was one of the first to publish Owen's poems.

Edith was interested in the interaction of poetry and music and this was published in a book called "Façade", first published in 1922.

This was a selection of abstract poems, set to music by William Walton. The poems were performed on stage, with a set consisting of a curtain on which was painted a face with a hole in place of the mouth – from which the sound of the poems came. The backcloth was painted by John Piper.

Her most famous poem, written during the Second World War was "Still Falls the Rain" about London during the Blitz. Benjamin Britten set this to music as "Canticle III: Still Falls The Rain".

In 1932 Edith and her governess moved to Paris until World War Two began when she returned to live in Renishaw with her brother Osbert. She spent her time knitting for friends who were serving in the Army. In 1954 she became a Dame Commander of the British Empire (OBE).

Edith claimed she wrote prose to earn a living. She wrote twenty collections of poetry and, among other prose books, two about Queen Elizabeth 1st and books about Queen Victoria, Alexander Pope and the city of Bath and also a novel called "I Live Under A Black Sun" about the life of Jonathan Swift.

From 1961 until her death in 1964, Edith lived in London. Her autobiography "Taken Care Of" was published posthumously.

Processions

WITHIN the long black avenues of Night
Go pageants of delight
With masks of glass the night has stained with wine,
Hair lifted like a vine;
And all the coloured curtains of the air
Were fluttered. Passing there,
The sounds seemed warring suns ; and music flowed
As blood ; the mask'd lamps showed
Tall houses, light had gilded like despair:
Black windows, gaping there.

Through all the rainbow spaces of our laughter
Those pageants followed after :
The negress Night, within her house of glass
Watched the processions pass.

The King Of China's Daughter

THE King of China's daughter
She never would love me,
Though I hung my cap and bells upon
Her nutmeg tree.
For oranges and lemons
The stars in bright blue air
(I stole them long ago, my dear)
Were dangling there.
The moon, she gave me silver pence ;
The sun did give me gold :
And both together softly blew
And made my porridge cold.
But the King of China's daughter
Pretended not to see,
When I hung my cap and bells upon
Her nutmeg tree.

Both poems first published in "Wheels – An Anthology Of Verse"
(Oxford: BH Blackwell, 1916)

Serenade Bergamasque

The Tremulous gold of stars within your hair
Are yellow bees flown from the hive at night
Finding the blossom of your eyes more fair
Than all the pae flowers folded from the light
Then, Sweet, awake and ope your dreaming eyes
Ere those bright bees have flown and darkness dies.

First published in "Wheels – Fourth Cycle" edited by Edith Sitwell
(Oxford: BH Blackwell, 1919)

CICELY FOX SMITH

Born 1ˢᵗ April 1882
in Lymm, Cheshire

Died 8ᵗʰ April 1954
Bow, Hampshire

Cicely attended Manchester High School for Girls from 1894 – 1897, writing poetry and describing herself as "something of a rebel". She published her first book of poems at the age of 17.

Cicely and her sister moved to Canada, where Cicely worked as a shorthand typist for the British Columbia Lands Department. She spent much of her spare time on the waterfront, which contributed to her knowledge of nautical matters, which was reflected in her poetry.

Cicely returned to England before 1914 and went to live in Hampshire with her sister. She wrote with such authority about the sea that many people supposed she was a man. In all, she published more than 630 poems in a wide variety of publications.

She also wrote novels, short stories and articles. At the age of 67 Cicely was awarded a pension by the Government 'for services to literature'. She died in Bow, Hampshire on 8ᵗʰ April 1954.

Farewell To Anzac

OH, hump your swag and leave, lads, the ships are in the bay;
We've got our marching orders now, it's time to come away;
And a long good-bye to Anzac beach where blood has flowed in
vain,
For we're leaving it, leaving it—game to fight again!

But some there are will never quit that bleak and bloody shore,
And some that marched and fought with us will fight and march no
more;
Their blood has bought till judgement day the slopes they stormed so
well,
And we're leaving them, leaving them, sleeping where they fell!
(Leaving them, leaving them, the bravest and the best;
Leaving them, leaving them, and maybe glad to rest!
We've done our best with yesterday, to-morrow's still our own—
But we're leaving them, leaving them, sleeping all alone!)

Ay, they are gone beyond it all, the praising and the blame,
And many a man may win renown, but none more fair a fame;
They showed the world Australia's lads knew well the way to die,
And we're leaving them, leaving them, quiet where they lie!
(Leaving them, leaving them, sleeping where they died;
Leaving them, leaving them, in their glory and their pride—
Round them sea and barren land, over them the sky,
Oh, we're leaving them, leaving them, quiet where they lie!

Previously published in "Fighting Men", (London: Elkin Matthews, 1916)

Next page: British Merchant Service
Previously published in "A Treasury of War Poetry – British And American poems of the world war 1914-17", edited by George Herbert Clarke. (Boston, USA: Houghton Mifflin, 1917).

British Merchant Service

Oh, down by Millwall Basin as I went the other day,
I met a skipper that I knew, and to him I did say:
"Now what's the cargo, Captain, that brings you up this way?"

"Oh, I've been up and down (said he) and round about also . . .
From Sydney to the Skagerack, and Kiel to Callao . . .
With a leaking steam-pipe all the way to Californ-i-o . . .

"With pots and pans and ivory fans and every kind of thing,
Rails and nails and cotton bales, and sewer pipes and string . . .
But now I'm through with cargoes, and I'm here to serve the King!

"And if it's sweeping mines (to which my fancy somewhat leans)
Or hanging out with booby-traps for the skulking submarines,
I'm here to do my blooming best and give the beggars beans!

"A rough job and a tough job is the best job for me,
And what or where I don't much care, I'll take what it may be,
For a tight place is the right place when it's foul weather at sea!"

There's not a port he doesn't know from Melbourne to New York;
He's as hard as a lump of harness beef, and as salt as pickled pork .
And he'll stand by a wreck in a murdering gale and count it part of his
work!

He's the terror of the fo'c'sle when he heals its various ills
With turpentine and mustard leaves, and poultices and pills . . .
But he knows the sea like the palm of his hand, as a shepherd
knows the hills.

He'll spin you yarns from dawn to dark—and half of 'em are true!
He swears in a score of languages, and maybe talks in two!
And . . . he'll lower a boat in a hurricane to save a drowning crew.

A rough job or a tough job—he's handled two or three—
And what or where he won't much care, nor ask what the risk may be
For a tight place is the right place when it's wild weather at sea!

MILLICENT SUTHERLAND

Born 20th October 1867
Fife, Scotland

Died 20th August 1955
Orriule, France

Note: Millicent Sutherland also used the
pen-name Erskine Gower

Millicent was born in Fife – the eldest daughter of Robert St. Clair-Erskine, Fourth Earl of Rosslyn and Blanche Adeliza Fitzroy, widow of the Hon. Charles Maynard.

On her 17th birthday (20th October 1884), Millicent married Lord Cromartie Sutherland-Leveson-Gower, Marquess of Stafford, the heir of the third Duke of Sutherland, a title which he inherited – along with the Trentham Hall Estate - on the death of his Father in 1892.

Millicent became a society hostess in London but also showed interest in the welfare of the pottery workers in Staffordshire. In 1900, she founded what would later become the "Duchess Of Sutherland Cripples Guild" which was charity to provide for child workers who had been injured in the potteries. Metalwork items were produced by the Guild and sold in a London showroom to raise funds and Millicent also compiled a book of poetry in 1904 to sell for the charity.

After the death of the Duke in 1913, Millicent married Major Desmond Percy Fitzgerald of the 11th Hussars in October 1914. At the outbreak of War, she funded and set up a Red Cross ambulance unit in France at the age of 46. Millicent was captured by the Germans in 1914 but escaped to Calais, where she managed the British Red Cross Hospital.

The French painter Victor Tardieu (1870 – 1937) who volunteered for the French Army in 1914, painted scenes of the hospital Millicent directed in the summer of 1915. These beautiful paintings have recently (March 2013) been purchased by the Florence Nightingale Museum.

Millicent moved to Roubaix in June 1918 with her Red Cross Unit. For her services during the First World War, Millicent was awarded the French Croix de Guerre, the Belgian Royal Red Cross and the British Red Cross Medal.

After the War, Millicent lived in France and was again captured in 1940. She escaped via Spain and Portugal and went to live in the United States of America, returning to Paris in 1945. She went to live in Orriule in South West France where she died in 1955.

No 2 of a series of 10 oil paintings by Victor Tardieu (1870-1937) entitled "The Camp In The Oat Field" and painted at Bourbourg during the Summer of 1915. This painting carries the dedication: " a Madame la Duchesse de Sutherland / Hommage respectueux et tres reconaisant d'un simple soldat."
More information and the rest of the paintings can be found at: www.milicentsutherlandambulance.com

The Tirailleur
(To the `memory of René)

He was so young to die - -
Ah; these are catwords now
When death sucks red lips white
Yet laurel-crowns the brow!

The while we slaked his thirst
Around us night-flies sang,
Why did we wish him life?
Why did we feel a pang?

He lived the night, to dawn,
And all the hot day through
The fever lit his eyes,
His limbs no resting knew.

"Je pars tout seul," he said.
Yet radiance on his face
Bespoke him radiant dreams
Veiled in eternal grace.

The hour he died, a moth
With golden quivering wings
Upon his pillow poised,
And whispered lovely things

To his dear fluttering soul - -
Of brothers at his side,
And comrades crying "Haste,
The boat is on the tide"- -

Till with the setting sun
Outward his spirit leapt - -
In calm the moon arose,
Only the Sister wept.

Millicent Sutherland

*First published in "The Fiery Cross: An Anthology". Edwards, Mabel C. and Booth,
Mary, Editors; (London: Grant Richards Ltd,1915).*

One Night

I walked into a moon of fold last night
Across grey sands she seemed to shine so bright.

Wide, wide the sands until I met the sea,
Cradle of moons, yet searchlights followed me.

I asked the moon if creeping round the Zones
She had seen good, or only poor things' bones.

"Pale faces I have seen, unconscious men
Bereft of struggling horror now and then.

"And sinking ships I see, and floating mines,
And cries I hear, "O God," and choking whines.

"But later when the stars shine on the wave
And give more light, I know the dead die brave.

"Passing so quickly from the things that count,
Count to all mortal thoughts, to find the Fount,

"Where angels pour elixir into bowls,
Drink, not for broken hearts, but thirsty souls."

"And what on shore?" I asked, "the great Divide
Where rivers run, and trenches side by side?"

"There", the moon said, "the snow was on the ground
And the frost pinched me as I beamed around.

"Red pools of gore, and ghastly shadows lay
In deep dug corners, so I sank away.

"Let misty cloudlets sweep across my face
To hide the earth, and give me heart of grace.

"Sudden the air seemed filled with eager breath
Of great Adventures, released from death,

"And shaking blood from out their eyes and hair
Shouting for further knowledge here and there.

"I lighted these across the treacherous Path
To reach the garden of Life's aftermath.

"And as they sped in troops the great guns boomed,
With flashes lightning swift, and dark hordes loomed,

"And phantom shapes of patient warrior bands - -
Then more snow fell and shrouded all the lands."

Now pondering from the moon I turned again,
Over the sands, back to our House of Pain.

Millicent Sutherland.

First published in "The Fiery Cross: An Anthology". Edwards, Mabel C. and Booth, Mary, Editors. (London: Grant Richards Ltd, 1915)

*A WW1 postcard entitled
"Duchess and Red Cross Nurses"
featuring Millicent Sutherand (far right).*

*These were sold to help raise funds for her
Calais war hospital.*

MARY WEBB

*Born 25th March 1881,
Leighton, Shropshire*

*Died 8th October 1927,
St Leonards –on-Sea, Sussex*

Mary was born Mary Gladys Meredith on 25th March 1881 in Leighton, near the Wrekin in Shropshire, 8 miles south west of Shrewsbury. Her father was a schoolmaster and he taught her at home, sending her to a finishing school in Southport.

Mary began writing poetry at an early age. She was awarded the "Femina Vie Heureuse" Award in 1925 for her book *Precious Bane*.

She married Henry Bertram Law Webb in 1912.

During the First World War, Mary lived near Pontesbury. She was deeply affected by the events of the First World War and was very worried about her three brothers

Mary suffered ill health and died at St. Leonards on Sea aged 46. She was buried in Shrewsbury. Her work began to be appreciated after her death – she was referred to as "the neglected genius".

There is now a Mary Webb Society and English musician Richard Moult has set several of Mary's poems to music and these can be found on his 2006 CD "The Secret Joy" released by Cynfeirdd (CYN040).

Like A Poppy On A Tower

Like a poppy on a tower
The present hour!
The wind stirs, the wind awakes,
Beneath its feet the tower shakes.
All down the crannied wall
Torn scarlet petals fall,
Like scattered fire or shivered glass
And drifting with their motion pass
Torn petals of blue shadow
From the grey tower to the green meadow

The Door

I heard humanity, through all the years,
Wailing, and beating on a dark, vast door
With urgent hands and eyes blinded by tears.
Will none come forth to them for evermore?
Like children at their father's door, who wait,
Crying 'Let us in!' on some bright birthday morn,
Quite sure of joy, they grow disconsolate,
Left in the cold unanswered and forlorn.
Forgetting even their toys in their alarms,
They only long to climb on father's bed
And cry their terrors out in father's arms.
And maybe, all the while, their father's dead.

Mary Webb

Both poems were previously published in "Poems and The Spring Of Joy" by Mary Webb (London: Jonathan Cape,1928).

DOWNE HOUSE SCHOOL GIRLS

POEMS WRITTEN BY PUPILS AT DOWNE HOUSE SCHOOL DURING THE FIRST WORLD WAR

These poems were kindly sent to us by Mrs Jennifer Kingsland, the Archivist at Downe House School, which was founded in 1907 as a girls' independent boarding school.

During the Great War, the school occupied a house in Kent that had previously belonged to Charles Darwin. The three poems reproduced here were originally published in the "Downe House School Magazine" in 1914.

A separate booklet featuring more poems by the girls at Downe House, as well as brief biographical details, is also available. See below for details.

A Fragment of Mr. Burns' Lectures

The kings who fought and won of old
Are made out grand and great,
Of deeds of chivalry we're told,
But books do not relate
How many men would kill a child to plunder,
And none were there to stay them or to wonder.
And you who raised the battle's din
Supposing, just, that you should win
And come in peace again,
D'you hope to cover over hearths made gory
Adjusting shiny bits of tinsel glory.

Olive Matthews, 1914

Alsace-Lorraine

At night in Alsace villages,
When women lie abed,
Come creeping through their lonely hearts
Dim phantoms of the dead.

When Alsace shall be free again,
The men who saved her pride,
Will wander back at night time
To the land for which they died.

They come to tread Alsatian soil
They gave their lives to free,
To look upon Alsatian girls
Who keep their memory.

When women hear a rustling
Against the window-pane,
And when they shiver in their dreams
'Tis the dead come back again.

Gaily and strong they face the fire,
And now that they are dead;
Back again to the land they loved,
Their ghostly steps are led.

At night in Alsace villages,
When Women lie abed,
Come creeping through their lonely hearts
Dim phantoms of the dead.

Audrey Lucas, 1914.

An English Victory

A Cavalry soldier is charging,
A Highlander runs by his side,
Both men are bent on enlarging
The gap in the hosts spreading wide.

Spreading wide in the Fair land of France
The mammoth-like hosts of the Huns,
Destroying with bayonet and lance,
With rifles and swords and with guns.

See how they fly in disorder,
Their hosts have diminished in size,
They fly as far as the border,
And vanish before our eyes.

They vanish for they are defeated,
Not a single soldier stands,
The Cavalry officer seated
On his horse, with his friend shakes hands.

Then may all the brave sons of Our Empire,
Who come from the country and street,
Desire their fame to rise higher,
And for Germany's army – defeat.

Irene Butler, 1914

LIVERPOOL POETS

Rachael Bates, Catherine Bridson and Catherine M. Jackson were kindly brought to my attention by Sheena Gaskell of the Birkenhead Reference Library. Some of their work was published in "Poets of Merseyside: An Anthology of Present-Day Liverpool Poetry", Edited by S. Fowler Wright and published by Merton Press Ltd., London, in 1923.

An extensive search has not, at the time of going to press, brought to light any significant biographical details for Bridson and Jackson, although we have found out some basic details about Rachel Bates.

Rachel Bates was born in 1897 to parents Joseph Ambrose Bates and Edith Annie Grimshaw. The family lived in lived in Great Crosby, Waterloo, Merseyside, where she worked as a secretary at The Liverpool Daily Post and Echo in their editorial department.

In 1922 she produced her first volume of poetry entitled "Danae And Other Poems" which was published by Erskine MacDonald Ltd, London WC1.

During the Second World War, Rachel moved to Sawrey in the Lake District where she continued to write poetry.

In 1947 she produced a collection of poems about her lakeland surroundings called "Songs From A Lake" which was published by Hutchinson.

She died in 1966 and is buried at St Michael & All Angels cemetery in Hawkshead.

Sea Change

Warehouses! That to commerce vowed
Still know the grace of sun and cloud,
Through pearly mist and slender rain
I read strange beauty in your plain
Void walls, a grey serenity
That's earnest of the quiet sea;
And when tempestuous morning dulls
The dark remembrance of your scars,
I see faint wings of shadowy gulls
Move in your gloom like phantom stars;
No footsteps mar that deep content
Nor any sound of human words,
But every roof is turbulent
With the long cry of wheeling birds.

I think the tides will rise one day
And leap about your grim array
With might of chill, translucent waves,
Charming your doorways into caves
Of magic, where the random flight
Shall penetrate your secret dreams

With bright, innumerable beams.
No longer shall your hoard comprise
A vain and transient merchandise,
But other treasurers richer far
Than tawny fruit of southern steeps –
The circling moon, the flying star –
Shall sow their harvest in your deeps.

Rachel Bates

Previously published in "Danae And Other Poems" by Rachel Bates
(London: Erskine MacDonald Ltd, 1922)

The Infinite Debt

A stranger died for me,
Groaned and dropped and died somewhere -
His fire quenched utterly
In a shrivelling air.

And how shall I requite
His wounds, his death, who dies unknown
And keeps my feeble flame alight
With ransom of his own?

All life, all love's his fee
Whose perished fire conserves his spark,
Who bought the brightening day for me
And for himself, the dark.

Rachel Bates

Previously published in "Poets of Merseyside: An Anthology of Present-Day Liverpool Poetry", Edited by S. Fowler Wright. (London: Merton Press Ltd,1923).

Peel Fishing Fleet

Bronze sail set to the bearing wind,
On wrack-strewn path, with foam-sprayed keel;
Borne on the ebbing, ev'ning tide,
Sets out the fishing fleet at Peel.

The setting sun half veils his light]
In grey dusk cloud and purple mist;
Foreshadowing what drear night-shades
Shall chill the waves – at noon sun-kissed.

Home with the dawning
Of a new morning;
The well-filled creels bring the spoils of the sea;
Nets on the field spread,
Pillow for tired head

Dreams of star silence and night's mystery.

Catherine Bridson

Previously published in "Poets of Merseyside: An Anthology of Present-Day Liverpool Poetry", Edited by S. Fowler Wright. (London: Merton Press Ltd, 1923).

Longing

Give me a bed of heather
There – with the smell of the sea,
And any kind of weather
Will do for a man like me.

If the North winds be singing
Their chant of the Vikings bold,
They will whip my face in passing,
As they to theirs of old.

If white the hail be flaying,
Or the mists begem my head,
I'll laugh at the elements playing,
As I lie on my purple bed.

Though the waves of the frenzied sea
Contend with the shrieking blast,
While they rise and fall in glee,
And their breath comes short and fast,

The while that the lightning flashes,
Cleaving the heavens in twain,
Through the sound of the battling crashes –
I laugh for the healing rain.

So give me a bed of heather,
Somewhere in sight of the sea,
And any kind of weather
Will do for a man like me

Catherine M. Jackson

Previously published in "Poets of Merseyside: An Anthology of Present-Day Liverpool Poetry", Edited by S. Fowler Wright. (London: Merton Press Ltd,1923).

PART TWO: USA & EMPIRE

"Anglo Saxon" designed by Henry Gates in 1898 as part of "Canada: Patriotics – The Wilson Series" for the JC Wilson & Company postcard manufacturers in Montreal, Canada.
More information can be found at www.jcwilson.ca

MOINA BELLE MICHAEL
UNITED STATES OF AMERICA

*Born 15th August 1869,
Good Hope, Georgia, USA*

*Died 10th May 1944,
Athens, Georgia, USA*

Known as "The Poppy Lady"

My research into Female Poets of the First World War led me to the wonderful website www.greatwar.co.uk which is sponsored and run by Rembrella Ltd. The following poem and the photograph of Moina Belle Michael are reproduced with kind permission of Rembrella Ltd.

Please have a look at the website to read the story behind Moina Belle Michael's poem "We shall keep the Faith" and how the poppy came to be adopted as the enduring symbol of The First World War on http://www.greatwar.co.uk/people/moina-belle-michael.htm

Moina Belle Michael, an American professor and humanitarian, was born in Georgia. At the outbreak of WW1, she was teaching at the University of Georgia but took leave of absence and went to New York to undertake the training of YMCA workers who were to be sent overseas.

After the war, Moina returned to Georgia and among her pupils were disabled ex-servicemen newly returned from fighting in the First World War.. First-hand experience of the aftermath of the Great War would have fuelled the idea of her poem:

Inspiration For The Poem
Having read John McCrae's poem **'In Flanders Fields'**, Moina Michael made a personal pledge to 'keep the faith'.

She felt compelled to make a note of this pledge and hastily scribbled down a response entitled "We Shall Keep the Faith" on the back of a used envelope. From that day she vowed to wear a red poppy of Flanders Fields as a sign of remembrance.

The idea soon spread through Moina's meetings with fellow members of the YMCA Secretaries of the Allied Nations and in 1919 the fledgling Royal British Legion in the UK adopted the poppy as its emblem.

Moina Belle Michael died in Athens, Georgia on 10th May 1944 and, 4 years later, was commemorated on a postage stamp.

In 1969, the Georgia General Assembly designated the stretch of US Highway 78 between Athens and Monroe the "Moina Michael Highway" in her honour.

We Shall Keep the Faith
by Moina Michael, November 1918

Oh! you who sleep in Flanders Fields,
Sleep sweet - to rise anew!
We caught the torch you threw
And holding high, we keep the Faith
With All who died.
We cherish, too, the poppy red
That grows on fields where valor led;
It seems to signal to the skies
That blood of heroes never dies,
But lends a lustre to the red
Of the flower that blooms above the dead
In Flanders Fields.
And now the Torch and Poppy Red
We wear in honor of our dead.
Fear not that ye have died for naught;
We'll teach the lesson that ye wrought
In Flanders Fields.

Previously published in "The Miracle Flower: The Story Of The Flanders Field Poppy" by Moina Belle Michael and Leonard Roan (Philadelphia: Dorrance & Co, 1941)

ELLA WHEELER WILCOX
UNITED STATES OF AMERICA

*Born 5th November 1850,
Johnstown, Wisconsin*

*Died 30th October 1919
Short Beach, Connecticut*

Ella was an American author and poet born in Johnstown, Wisconsin in 1850. Ella was the youngest of four children. Her family moved to Madison soon after her birth. Ella began writing poetry at a very early age and by the time she graduated from her high school, she already had a reputation as a poet within the State of Wisconsin.

Ella was known as "The Poetess of Passion" and her most famous poem, "Solitude", was published on 25th February 1898 in "The New York Sun". Apparently, inspiration for that poem came to Ella while she was travelling to the Governor of Madison's Inaugural Ball.

Ella married Robert Wilcox of Meriden, Connecticut in 1884 and they moved to Short Beach, Branford, Connecticut, near Long Island where they built several houses and held social gatherings bringing together the stars of the literary and artistic world of the time. The couple travelled extensively, throughout Europe and Asia.

Ella was a strong swimmer and organised swimming competitions in Short Beach. She was also very interested in spiritualism and helped to found the Rosicrucian Order in America.

After more than thirty years of marriage, Ella's husband died in 1916 and she was filled with despair.

It could be this feeling of despair that drove Ella to work tirelessly for the cause when America entered the First World War.

According to her biography, Ella, who with her husband was a fan of "New Age" philosophies including Occultism, explained that Robert had communicated with her through a Ouija Board and had instructed her to go to France to help.

She travelled to France 'as the representative of The Red Star Animal Relief Programme', which was founded in August 1916 to help animals used by the American Army during WW1. That organisation is today called Animal Emergency Services. Ella also helped out with entertaining the troops, visiting camps and hospitals and reading the soldiers poems she wrote while in France. Ella kept these verses deliberately simple in order to appeal to a wide audience. She also lectured the troops on the importance of taking care during sexual encounters in a series of tours of Allied army camps. Her poem "The Price He Paid" was made into a silent film in 1914.

The poems Ella wrote in France were collected into a special volume of her work called "Hello, Boys!".

Travelling to France would be quite an undertaking for a woman of 68 on her own now, let alone in those days before passenger plane flights and before the days of luxury cruise liners. During her work with the troops in France, Ella fell ill and returned home to Short Beach where she died in October 1919.

Ella published more than 70 books - poems (of which she wrote thousands), songs, plays and magazine articles, including "The Worlds and I" her autobiography which was published in 1919. Some of her poems were put to music by famous composers. Ella was also an accomplished singer and musician and she played the mandolin.

My own Father was always quoting the first line of Ella's most famous poem to me so I am including it here as it has a very special message.

Solitude

Laugh, and the world laughs with you;
Weep, and you weep alone.
For the sad old earth must borrow it's mirth,
But has trouble enough of its own.
Sing, and the hills will answer;
Sigh, it is lost on the air.
The echoes bound to a joyful sound,
But shrink from voicing care.

Rejoice, and men will seek you;
Grieve, and they turn and go.
They want full measure of all your pleasure,
But they do not need your woe.
Be glad, and your friends are many;
Be sad, and you lose them all.
There are none to decline your nectared wine,
But alone you must drink life's gall.

Feast, and your halls are crowded;
Fast, and the world goes by.
Succeed and give, and it helps you live,
But no man can help you die.
There is room in the halls of pleasure
For a long and lordly train,
But one by one we must all file on
Through the narrow aisles of pain.

First published on 25th February 1898 in "The New York Sun".

Belgium

Ruined? destroyed? Ah, no; though blood in rivers ran
Down all her ancient streets; though treasures manifold
Love-wrought, Time-mellowed, and beyond the price of gold
Are lost, yet Belgium's star shines still in God's vast plan.

Rarely have Kings been great, since kingdoms first began;
Rarely have great kings been great men, when all was told.
But, by the lighted torch in mailed hands, behold,
Immortal Belgium's immortal king, and Man.

First published in "King Albert's Book – a tribute to the Belgian king and people from representative men and women throughout the world" compiled by William Dean Howells (New York: Hearst's International Library Co. 1914)

Greater Britain

Our hearts were not set on fighting,
We did not pant for the fray,
And whatever wrongs need righting,
We would not have met that way.
But the way that has opened before us
Leads on thro' a blood-red field;
And we swear by the great God o'er us,
We will die, but we will not yield.

The battle is not of our making,
And war was never our plan;
Yet, all that is sweet forsaking,
We march to it, man by man.
It is either to smite, or be smitten,
There's no other choice to-day;
And we live, as befits the Briton,
Or we die, as the Briton may.

We were not fashioned for cages,
Or to feed from a keeper's hand;
Our strength which has grown thro' ages

Is the strength of a slave-free land.
We cannot kneel down to a master,
To our God alone can we pray;
And we stand in this world disaster,
To fight, like a lion at bay.

Mobilisation

Oh the Kings of earth have mobilised their men.
See them moving, valour proving,
To the fields of glory going,
Banners flowing, bugles blowing,
Every one a mother's son,
Brave with uniform and gun,
Keeping step with easy swing,
Yes, with easy step and light marching onward to the fight,
Just to please the warlike fancy of a King;
Who has mobilised his army for the strife.

Oh the King of Death has mobilised his men.
See the hearses huge and black
How they rumble down the track;
With their coffins filled with dead,
Filled with men who fought and bled;
Now from fields of glory coming
To the sound of muffled drumming
They are lying still and white,
But the Kings have had their fight;
Death has mobilised his army for the grave.

Both poems first published in "Poems Of Optimism" by Ella Wheeler Wilcox (London: Gay & Hancock, 1915)

LENA GUILBERT FORD
UNITED STATES OF AMERICA

Born 1870, Pennsylvania, USA

Died 7th March 1918, London

Lena Guilbert Brown was born in Venango County, Pennsylvania, America and attended the Elmira College in New York State.

She married Harry Hale Ford and they lived in Elmira. After their divorce, Lena moved with her Son and Mother to live in London, where they remained for twenty years.

Lena met Ivor Novello with whom she collaborated to write the lyrics for the song "Keep the Home Fires Burning". Other lyrics by Lena are "We Are Coming, Mother England", "When God Gave You To Me" and "God Guard You".

On 7th March 1918, Lena and her son were killed during a German air raid on London. They were the first American civilian casualties to be killed in an air raid in London during the First World.

Mrs Brown was slightly injured during the raid but survived. The bodies of Lena and her son were returned to the United States for burial.

Bombing Raids on Civilian Targets during WW1
There appears to be scant public knowledge of the air raids that took place in the UK during the First World War. Most people know about the bombardment of Scarborough, Hartlepool and Whitby from the sea on 16th December 1914 by German Battlecruisers but there were also Zeppelin raids during the First World War and later bombs were dropped from Gotha GV bomber planes.

An eye witness who was five years old and living in South London was witness to a burning Zeppelin and described how women came out of their houses shaking their fists and shouting obscenities at the burning airship.

In September 1916, Zeppelin raids on the UK were scaled back in favour of Gothas and the first air raid by Gotha Gv bombers took place in May 1917.

The last Zeppelin raid was in August 1918 when 4 airships bombed targets in the Midlands and the North of England.

Poet Robert Ross wrote to Siegfried Sassoon describing a bombing raid on London:

"One night I found an unhappy old woman bent double with age making unhappy dives across the road in Piccadilly just as the guns had begun firing. I took her to the Ritz Hotel & asked if they would allow her to wait in the hall, this was refused on the ground of her dirt and miserable appearance!! With some difficulty I got her to the Dover Street tube. I wrote to the authorities on the matter & I am bound to recount that the Ritz has now a notice board out "Refuge in Air Raids". I observe a different porter to the one who refused us admission."

A German Gotha V Bomber depicted on a WW1 Postcard

Keep the Home Fires Burning

They were summoned from the hillside
They were called in from the glen,
And the country found them ready
At the stirring call for men.
Let no tears add to their hardships
As the soldiers pass along,
And although your heart is breaking
Make it sing this cheery song:

(*Chorus*) Keep the Home Fires Burning,
While your hearts are yearning,
Though your lads are far away
They dream of home.
There's a silver lining
Through the dark clouds shining,
Turn the dark cloud inside out
'Til the boys come home.

Overseas there came a pleading,
"Help a nation in distress."
And we gave our glorious laddies
Honour bade us do no less,
For no gallant son of freedom
To a tyrant's yoke should bend,
And a noble heart must answer
To the sacred call of "Friend."

Repeat Chorus

(Lyrics by Lena Gilbert Brown Ford, Music by Ivor Novello)
Published in London by Ascherberg, Hopwood & Crew 1914.

GRACE D VANAMEE
UNITED STATES OF AMERICA

Born 1876, Connecticut, USA

*Died 10th December 1946,
New York, USA*

Grace was Administrative assistant to the President of the National Institute of Arts and Letters and the American Academy of Arts and Letters from 1915 to 1940. She was a feminist and womens' suffrage leader and was treasurer of the Women's National Republican Club and editor of "The Guidon" from 1927 to 1930.

She wrote a biography of former US President Theodore Roosevelt, which was published in 1919.

Grace wrote the following poem about the death of the American poet/singer Alan Seeger, uncle of Pete Seeger. Alan joined the French Foreign Legion in August 1914 as America had not yet joined the conflict at that time.

US Postcard from 1905 celebrating the "Portsmouth Treaty" where America President Theodore Roosevelt successfully negotiated an end ot the Russo- Japanese war.

Grace Vanamee later wrote a biogrpahy of this popular US President.

The Sequel: He Kept His Rendezvous With Death

"After reading "I have a Rendezvous with Death" by Alan Seeger,
who was killed in battle at Belloy-en-Santerre in July, 1916"

He kept his rendezvous with Death
At fateful Belloy-en-Santerre,
Though Spring had passed all unaware
And Summer scents were in the air.
He kept his rendezvous with Death,
He whose young life had been a prayer.

We strain our eyes the way he went,
Our soldier-singer, Heaven-sent,
We strain our eyes and catch our breath
But he has slipped from out our sight;
He kept his rendezvous with Death
And then emerged into the light
Of that fair day that yet may be
For those who conquer as did he.

God knows twas hard for him to go
From all he loved - to make that choice,
And leave for them such bitter woe!
But his hight courage was his breath,
And with his greatest work undone

He kept his rendezvous with Death.
Brave Hero-Poet we rejoice
That Life and Art with you were one,
That you to your own songs were true:
You did not fail that rendezvous!

Grace D Vanamee

First published in the magazine "The Art World" in January 1917, Volume 1, No. 4
and is reproduced here by kind permission of Matt Jacobsen, Editor of the website
www.oldmagazinearticles.com

JEAN BLEWETT
CANADA

Born 4th November 1872 at Scotia, Ontario

Died 19th August 1934 Chatham, Ontario

Pen name: Katherine Kent

Jean (nee McKishnie) was born in Canada in 1872. Both her parents were Scottish by birth. In 1889, Jean married Bassett Blewett who hailed from Cornwall.

From an early age, Jean began to write poems, essays and short stories and to have them published. She published her first novel in 1890 and her first volume of poems in 1897. One of her poems won the Chicago Times-Herald Prize.

The story behind this poem is given as follows:

Royal Navy Air Service pilot Lieutenant Reginald Warneford, while patrolling the skies over Belgium in his aeroplane at 3 o'clock in the morning of June 7th, 1915, destroyed a German armed Zeppelin, containing twenty-eight men.

The young aviator won instant fame by his heroic act. He received the Victoria Cross from King George and the Legion of Honour from France.

In sad irony, he was killed the same day he received his French medal, on 17th June as his plane crashed while taking a journalist on a non-combat mission.

What Time The Morning Stars Arise

ABOVE him spreads the purple sky,
Beneath him spreads the ether sea,
And everywhere about him lie
Dim ports of space, and mystery.

Ho, lonely Admiral of the Fleet!
What of the night? What of the night?
'Methinks I hear,' he says, 'the beat
Of great wings rising for the flight.'

Ho, Admiral neighbouring with the stars
Above the old world's stress and din!
With Jupiter and lordly Mars—
'Ah, yonder sweeps a Zeppelin!

A bird with menace in its breath,
A thing of peril, spoil and strife,
The little children done to death,
The helpless old bereft of life.

The moan of stricken motherhood,
The cowardice beyond our ken,
The cruelty that fires the blood,
And shocks the souls of honest men.

These call for vengeance—mine the chase.
He guides his craft—elate and strong.
Up, up, through purple seas of space,
While in his heart there grows a song.

'Ho, little ship of mine that soars
Twixt earth and sky, be ours to-day
To free our harassed seas and shores
Of yonder evil bird of prey!'

The gallant venture is his own,
No friend to caution, pray, or aid,
But strong is he who fights alone,
Of loss and failure unafraid.

He rises higher, higher still,
Till poised above the startled foe—
It is a fight to stir and thrill
And set the dullest breast aglow.

Old Britain hath her battles won
On fields that are a nation's pride,
And oh the deeds of daring done
Upon her waters deep and wide!

But warfare waged on solid land,
Or on the sea, can scarce compare
With this engagement, fierce, yet grand,
This duel to the death in air.

He wins! he wins in sea of space!
Why prate we now of other wars
Since he has won his name and place
By deathless valour 'mong the stars?

No more that Zeppelin will mock,
No more will sound her song of hate;
With bursting bomb, and fire, and shock,
She hurtles downward to her fate.

A touch of rose in eastern skies,
A little breeze that calls and sings,
Look yonder where our hero flies,
Like homing bird on eager wings.

He sees the white mists softly curl,
He sees the moon drift pale and wan,
Sees Venus climb the stairs of pearl
To hold her court of Love at dawn.

Jean Blewett

Previously published in "Canadian Poets" edited by John William Garvin (Toronto: McClelleland, Goodchild & Stewart, 1916)

ALICE GORE-JONES
AUSTRALIA

Born 29ʰ May 1887
Toowong, Queensland

Died 26ʰ July 1961
Brisbane, Queensland

Alice was born in Toowong, near Brisbane, in Queensland, Austraia to an Irish father Australian mother.

She was educated in Queensland, and New South Wales, Australia. Her first poems were published in 1904 and she continued writing until her death. Alice's only anthology of poems – "Troop Trains" - was published in 1917.

Alice was a poet and also worked as a columnist for several Brisbane newspapers, among them the "Courier Mail" and "Telegraph". She never married.

The Lists

These are the lists of death:
They were so young!
Brave valiant hearts
Who loved the earth and sun,
The stir of life,
And joy's swift ardent breath.
These are the lists:
When shall their memory fade?

The nation's best beloved of her sons,
Her shining, high, immortal, steadfast ones;
Honour, not death,
Has sealed their accolade.

Troop Trains

Troop trains troop trains
Passing on their way.
A sudden gust of cheering cuts
The crisp cold winter's day.

Above, a sky swept clear of cloud,
A blue infinity;
Below, the dun-brown carriages
Steaming towards the quay.

All along the railway line,
Where the people dwell,
Flecks of eager handkerchiefs
Fluttering in farewell.

Troop trains, troops trains,
Hear the bugle's note,
Flags, and cheers, and music, and...
A touch that grips the throat.

Both poems previously published in "Troop Trains" by Alice Gore-Jones (Adelaide: Hassell, 1917)

EMILY BULCOCK
AUSTRALIA

Born 28th July 1877
Mayborough, Queensland

Died 6th September 1969
Brisbane, Queensland

Photo by Mary Lambert

Emily was born Emily Hemans Palmer at Tinana, near Maryborough in Queensland. Her Father was a schoolteacher and her brother, Vance, became a writer. Emily began having her poems published at the age of 12 and in 1898, "The Queenslander" newspaper began publishing her poems.

Emily became a schoolteacher and married Robert Bulcock in 1903. Her first volume of poetry was published in 1923 – "Jacaranda Blooms" and she continued writing until her death.

When Emily died at the age of 92 in 1969, the "Courier Mail", a Brisbane newspaper, described her as "Queensland's unofficial poetess laureate"

At Toowong
Unveiling of Anzac Memorial, Sunday July 2, 1922

They met to honour the brave young dead,
Where a noble shaft rose high!
In the quiet park – on a grassy knoll,
Remembering those who paid the toll
And showed men how to die!

The ghost of a brave young moon looked down
Through the Sabbath calm and peace!
Scarcely a whisper the silence broke –
Till, solemn and deep the great drum spoke
And gave our thoughts release.

And the grand old hymns that in war and peace
Have set men's hearts afire!
Went floating up to the listening sky!
And curious flocks of birds came by,
As if to join the choir!

As tho' our wealth of loving thoughts
Had warmed the sullen day.
God lent His sun a little space,
It touched the scene with tender grace,
And chased all gloom away.

A-near the branching eucalypts –
Line of blue hills afar!
They spoke of loyalty, honour, truth!
And back came troops of radiant youth!
Death set its gates ajar.

How oft those boyish feet had trod
These very paths along!
Had scaled Mount Coot-tha's splendid height,
Or skimmed with outspread sails of white,
The river at Toowong.

Love brought its wealth of immortelles,
Pure white, as for a bride!
But who could see, untouched, unmoved,
The Wattles from the trees they loved,
Those boyish names beside?

And like a prayer made visible
We saw with reverence there
Man's loving thoughts set firm in stone!
Ah lads! the peace you long have known
Hushed all our hearts to prayer!

Published in "Jacaranda Blooms" by Emily Hemans Bulcock
(Brisbane: The Queensland Book Depot, 1923)

SAROJINI NAIDU
INDIA

Born 13rd February 1879
Hyderabad, India

Died 2nd March 1949
Lucknow, Uttar Pradesh, India

Known as the Nightingale Of India

Sarojini Chattopadhyay was born in Hyderabad on 13th February 1879. She was the eldest of a large family and learnt English when she was small. When she was twelve years old, she passed the Matriculation Examination of Madras University.

Sarojini wanted to marry Dr. Govindurajulu Naidu, who though from a well-established and esteemed family, was not from the same Caste as Sarojini's family. In the hopes that she would forget about Dr Naidu, her family sent her to England to continue her studies.

In 1895 she went to study at King's College, London and later she went to Girton College, Cambridge. She remained in England for three years, except for a brief sejour in Italy. During her stay in England, Sarojini met Arthur Symons, a poet and critic with whom she corresponded when she returned to India and who persuaded her to publish her poems.

In December 1898, Sarojini caused scandal in India because she married Dr. Naidu, thus breaking through the bonds of the Caste system in India. In 1916, Sarojini met Mahatma Ghandi and from then on devoted her energy to the cause of Independence. She was also a feminist and travelled from State to State urging Indian women to leave the kitchen and campaigning for women's rights. In 1928 she travelled to the USA.

After Independence, Sarojini became Governor of Uttar Pradesh. She was the first woman to become President of the Indian National Congress.

She died on 2nd March 1949.

To The God Of Pain

Unwilling priestess in thy cruel fane,
Long hast thou held me, pitiless god of Pain,
Bound to thy worship by reluctant vows,
My tired breast girt with suffering, and my brows
Anointed with perpetual weariness.
Long have I borne thy service, through the stress
Of rigorous years, sad days and slumberless nights,
Performing thine inexorable rites.

For thy dark altars, balm nor milk nor rice,
But mine own soul thou'st ta'en for sacrifice:
All the rich honey of my youth's desire,
And all the sweet oils from my crushed life drawn,
And all my flower-like dreams and gem-like fire
Of hopes up-leaping like the light of dawn.

I have no more to give, all that was mine
Is laid, a wrested tribute, at thy shrine;
Let me depart, for my whole soul is wrung,
And all my cheerless orisons are sung;
Let me depart, with faint limbs let me creep
To some dim shade and sink me down to sleep.

Sarojini Naidu

Originally published in "The Golden Threshold" by Sarojini Naidu
(London: William Heinemann, 1905)

EDITH LM KING
South Africa

Born 1871 In Pietermaritzburg

Died 1962

Edith Louise Marie King was born in Pietermaritzberg, Natal, South Africa in 1871. She studied in England and then went to Paris to study art.

She became a schoolteacher and was later Headmistress at the Eunice High School in Bloemfontein until she retired in 1922.

Cattle in Trucks

Poor cows, poor sheep,
I weep, I weep
To see you packed so tight;
While nought you know
Of where you go
By empty day and night.

Such noise, such heat,
Such weary feet,
No single thing you know.
No rest, no grass,
Only alas!
Your friends as scared as you.

I wish, I wish,
O how I wish,
That you could understand
That all is well;
You go to dwell
In some far pasture land.

PART THREE: REST OF THE WORLD

"Pour Le Drapeau Pour la Victoire" by Georges Scott (1873-1942)
Published in 1917 by Devampez Imp, Paris.

MARIE NIZET
BELGIUM

Born 19th January 1859
Brussels, Belgium

Died 15th March 1922
Etterbeek, Belgium

Marie was Belgian. It was because Belgium was threatened with occupation by the German Army that the British Expeditionary Force went there in 1914.

Marie was born in Brussels in Belgium, Her father Francois-Joseph was a writer and poet and worked for the Royal Library in Brussels. Marie was interested in Russia and Rumania and her work reflected this.

When she was studying in Paris she mixed with Rumanians, which probably fuelled her interest in Rumanian mythology. Marie's book "Captain Vampire" was published when she was 19 years old – 17 years before Bram Stoker's book was published.

Marie married, was divorced and brought her son up alone. She died in 1922.

Fins Derniers (trans: Final Endings)

C'est fête aujourd'hui, mon amour,
Je viens frapper à votre porte.
Notre bonheur est de retour :
Vous êtes mort et je suis morte.

Faites-moi, dans ce lit sans draps,
Une place, que je me couche

Entre ce qui fut vos deux bras,
Près de ce qui fut votre bouche.

Nous allons à deux nous plonger
Dans le Grand Tout qui nous réclame
Nos corps vont se désagréger
Pour un effroyable amalgame.

Notre chair, lambeau par lambeau,
Va se dissoudre en pourriture,
Reprise, à travers le tombeau,
Par le creuset de la nature ;

Nos os, par un beau soir d'été,
Tomberont les uns sur les autres...
Ne plus savoir — ô volupté ! —
Quels sont les miens, quels sont les vôtres !

À leur tour ils s'effriteront
En une impalpable poussière
Et tels, enfin, ils monteront
Dans un infini de lumière.

Nos atomes purifiés,
Emportés par le vent qui passe,
Comme en des vols extasiés,
S'éparpilleront dans l'espace.

Et sous les évolutions
D'éternelles métamorphoses
Nous danserons dans les rayons
Où nous ferons fleurir les roses.

Previously published in "Pour Axel De Missie" by Marie Mercier-Nizet
(Brussels: Editions De La Vie Intellectuelle, 1923)

La Torche (trans: The Torch)

Je vous aime, mon corps, qui fûtes son désir,
Son champ de jouissance et son jardin d'extase
Où se retrouve encor le goût de son plaisir
Comme un rare parfum dans un précieux vase.

Je vous aime, mes yeux, qui restiez éblouis
Dans l'émerveillement qu'il traînait à sa suite
Et qui gardez au fond de vous, comme en deux puits,
Le reflet persistant de sa beauté détruite.

Je vous aime, mon coeur, qui scandiez à grands coups
Le rythme exaspéré des amoureuses fièvres,
Et mes pieds nus noués aux siens et mes genoux
Rivés à ses genoux et ma peau sous ses lèvres...

Je vous aime ma chair, qui faisiez à sa chair
Un tabernacle ardent de volupté parfaite
Et qui preniez de lui le meilleur, le plus cher,
Toujours rassasiée et jamais satisfaite.

Et je t'aime, ô mon âme avide, toi qui pars
- Nouvelle Isis - tentant la recherche éperdue
Des atomes dissous, des effluves épars
De son être où toi-même as soif d'être perdue.

Je suis le temple vide où tout culte a cessé
Sur l'inutile autel déserté par l'idole;
Je suis le feu qui danse à l'âtre délaissé,
Le brasier qui n'échauffe rien, la torche folle...

Et ce besoin d'aimer qui n'a plus son emploi
Dans la mort, à présent retombe sur moi-même.
Et puisque, ô mon amour, vous êtes tout en moi
Résorbé, c'est bien vous que j'aime si je m'aime

Previously published in "Pour Axel De Missie" by Marie Mercier-Nizet
(Brussels: Editions De La Vie Intellectuelle, 1923)

GABRIELA MISTRAL
CHILE

Born 7th April 1889,
Vicuna, Chile

Died 10th January 1957,
Hempstead, NY, USA

Note: Gabriela Mistral was the pen name of
Lucila Godoy Alcayaga

Born in Vicuna, Chile in 1889. Her father left the family when she was three hers old. By the time she was sixteen, Gabriela was supporting her mother by working as a classroom assistant. In 1906, she met Romeo Ureta who became the love of her life.

Romeo's death in 1909 left Gabriela depressed and this was compounded by the death of her nephew at the age of seventeen.

Gabriela was able to have a successful career in education and published books about education and collections of her poetry.

She took part in the organisation of education in Mexico and Chile and played an active part in cultural committees of the League of Nations. She was Chilean Consul in Naples, Madrid and Lisbon, and held honorary degrees from the Universities of Florence and Guatemala. She taught Spanish Literature at Columbia University, Middlebury College and Vassar College and at the University of Puerto Rico.

In 1945 Gabriela received the Nobel Prize for Literature and she was the first Latin American female poet to be awarded this prize - the Citation reads: "for her lyric poetry which, inspired by powerful emotions, has made her name a symbol of the idealistic aspirations of the entire Latin American world".

Gabriela died in 1957.

El Dios Triste (trans: The Sad God)

Mirando la alameda de otoño lacerada,
la alameda profunda de vejez amarilla,
como cuando camino por la hierba segada
busco el rostro de Dios y palpo su mejilla.

Y en esta tarde lenta como una hebra de llanto
por la alameda de oro y de rojez yo siento
un Dios de otoño, un Dios sin ardor y sin canto
¡y lo conozco triste, lleno de desaliento!

Y pienso que tal vez Aquel tremendo y fuerte
Señor, al que cantara de locura embriagada,
no existe, y que mi Padre que las mañanas vierte
tiene la mano laxa, la mejilla cansada.

Se oye en su corazón un rumor de alameda
de otoño: el desgajarse de la suma tristeza.
Su mirada hacia mí como lágrima rueda
y esa mirada mustia me inclina la cabeza.

Y ensayo otra plegaria para este Dios doliente,
plegaria que del polvo del mundo no ha subido:
"Padre, nada te pido, pues te miro a la frente
y eres inmenso, ¡inmenso!, pero te hallas herido".

Previously published in "Desolacion - Poemas" by Gabriela Mistral
(New York: Instituto de las Espanas en Estados Unidos, 1922)

BING XIN 冰心
CHINA

Born 5th December 1900,
Fuzhou, Fujian, China

Died 28th February 1999,
Bejing, China

Bing Xin was born in Fuzhou, Fujian, China. Her family moved to Yantai, Shandong when she was aged four years. Living by the sea had a profound impact on the young girl. In 1913, the family moved to Beijing and The May the Fourth Movement of 1919 was also pivotal in Bing Xin's life. She wrote for her school magazine and published her first novel.

Bing Xin studied literature at Janjing University and went to the USA to do a Master's Degree at Wellesley College in Massachusetts.

She married Wu Werzao an anthropologist and together they travelled the world. Bing Xin wrote a large amount of poetry, children's books, essays, novels and reviews. She is loved, revered and respected in China and when she died thousands of people turned out with red roses - her favourite flower - to pay their respects to their favourite author.

The Commonwealth War Graves Commission has published a pamphlet about The Chinese Labour Corps at the Western Front. Due to the terrible loss of life, by 1916 the Allies needed unskilled labour to support the army behind the Trenches.

China remained neutral but agreed to the format of the Chinese Labour Corps. The Corps was non-combatant but part of the British Army and under their control.

They were to carry out manual duties such as building and repairing roads, railways and airfields and unloading ships and trains. As time went on, they became more skilled and carried out repairs to vehicles and tanks.

By the end of 1917, there were 54,000 Chinese labourers working alongside the Commonwealth Forces in France and Belgium, recruited from the resident Chinese populations of Canada and other Allied countries after China entered the War in August 1917. The Chinese quickly earned a reputation for hard work, ingenuity and improvisation. By the end of the War, the Corps had almost 96,000 members and after the Armistice, they undertook the very difficult, dangerous and unpleasant task of clearing the battlefield.

Infinite Stars

The infinite stars are twinkling—
The dark blue sky,
Why have I never heard their whispers?
In the tranquility,
And in the eclipsed light,
They express their encomiums sincerely.

O! My childhood,
Is the truth of dream,
Is the dream of truth,
Is the smile with tears while recollecting.

With the vast fields quivering—
Beside the darkened black island,
The moon is coming up,
The fountainhead of life,
The hideout for death

O! My little brothers,
The three little joyful stars of my spirit,
Brings me brightness.
My love in the deep soul,
I loved them speechlessly.

Darkness,
How can it be depicted?
In the depth of the soul,
The depth of the cosmos,
And at the stop
Of the resplendent radiance.

The mirror
Reflects me face to face,
However, I feel it to be unnatural.
Better to turn it around!

Awakening, I hear
Only the indignant hermits,
Listening to
The gongs breaking the fatal fates.

On the lush branches,
The withered remains survive;
The birds have vanished away.
Falling flowers scatter all about—
Isn't life the same as this glance?

Dreams are the least ones to deceive,
Clearly,
Honestly,
It implies
The hidden interpretation
And the secret worry

In your soul.

First published 1921

In the preface to "Infinite Stars", Bing Xin explains that rather than being poetry as such, this volume is a gathering together of various random thoughts and ideas that she often had and noted down but was unable to complete or find any particular use for. Her younger brothers suggested that she set them out on paper and publish them and the result was "Infinite Stars" – a collection of 164 "verselets", of which just the first few are reproduced here.

EDITH SŐDERGRAN

Finland

Born 4th April 1892
St Petersberg, Russia

Died 24th June 1923
Raivola, Finnish Karelia

During the First World War, Finland was still part of Russia and the Finnish Army was part of the Russian Army. After the Revolution in 1917, Finland declared independence in December 1917. Sweden remained neutral during WW1.

Edith Irene Södergran a Swedish-speaking Finnish poet. She was born in St. Petersburg, Russia to a middle-class couple – Matts Sődergran and Helena (nee Holmroos) who were born in Finland but spoke Swedish at their mother tongue. The family moved to live in Raivola on the Karelian Isthmus when Edith was still a baby.

Edith went to a school in St Petersburg opposite the Winter Palace. She was a keen photographer.

In 1904 Edith's father contracted TB and he died when she was fifteen. Soon afterwards, Edith herself was diagnosed with the disease and was sent to a sanitorium. In 1911, Edith and her Mother travelled to Switzerland for treatment where she met many inspirational people.

Edith's first volume of poems – "Dikter" (Poems) - was published in 1916 but her unusual modern style did not meet with great success.

Edith's illness, the poverty that dogged her life and the parallel unrest in the world at the time of the First World War and the Russian Revolution undoubtedly had an effect on her writing. She stopped writing between 1920 and 1922 and then, inspired by a magazine called "Ultra" devoted to literary modernism in Finland, she wrote her final poems.

She died in Raivola on 23rd June 1923 and was buried in the village churchyard.   The area became part of the Soviet Union after the Second World War and Raivola is now called Roschino.

Edith is considered to be a "trailblazer" within modernist Swedish poetry and her poems have since been translated into Russian, Spanish and Chinese. A statue of her was erected in Raivola in 1960.

Nocturne

Moonlit evening, silver clear
and the night's blue billows,
sparkling waves, numberless,
follow one another.
Shadows fall along the path,
on the shore the bushes softly weep,
black giants guard its silver in their keep.
Silence deep in summer's midst,
sleep and dream, -
the moon glides out across the sea
white tender gleam.

A Wish

Of all our sunny world
I wish only for a garden sofa
where a cat is sunning itself.
There I should sit
with a letter at my breast,
a single small letter.
That is what my dream looks like.

Both poems first published in "Dikter" by Edith Södergran.
(Borga / Porvoo: Holger Schildts Forlag, 1916)

LUCIE DELARUE–MARDRUS
France

*Born 3rd November 1874
in Honfleur, Normandy*

*Died 26th April 1945
Château – Gontier, France*

Lucie was a French poet. She was born in Honfleur on the coast of Normandy in France. Her Father, Georges Delarue, was a lawyer.

Lucie was very talented, being apart from a poet, a prolific writer, journalist, sculptor and designer. She was married to the translator and expert in oriental studies J.C. Mardrus from 1900 until 1915, and until the outbreak of war, Lucie wrote extensively, became famous and travelled the world.

The couple separated and divorced in 1915 and Lucie was able to follow her heart and become openly lesbian. She lived and worked in Paris until 1936 when she moved to Chateau-Gontier in Mayenne, North West France.

Lucie was a fine horsewoman and also played chess. She wrote more than 70 books, novels, biographies and plays and also acted in her plays. At the outbreak of the First World War, Lucie, who volunteered as a nurse in Honfleur Hospital 13 during the war, wrote:

> Toi mère et toi, ma sœur Marie
> Pour moi récitez un Ave
> Allons enfants de la patrie
> Le jour de gloire est arrivé

16th August 1914.

L'Automne

On voit tout le temps, en automne,
Quelque chose qui vous étonne,
C'est une branche, tout à coup,
Qui s'effeuille dans votre cou.
C'est un petit arbre tout rouge,
Un, d'une autre couleur encor,
Et puis, partout, ces feuilles d'or
Qui tombent sans que rien ne bouge.
Nous aimons bien cette saison,
Mais la nuit si tôt va descendre !
Retournons vite à la maison
Rôtir nos marrons dans la cendre.

L'Odeur De Mon Pays...

L'odeur de mon pays était dans une pomme.
Je l'ai mordue avec les yeux fermés du somme,
Pour me croire debout dans un herbage vert.
L'herbe haute sentait le soleil et la mer,
L'ombre des peupliers y allongeaient des raies,
Et j'entendais le bruit des oiseaux, plein les haies,
Se mêler au retour des vagues de midi...

Combien de fois, ainsi, l'automne rousse et verte
Me vit-elle, au milieu du soleil et, debout,
Manger, les yeux fermés, la pomme rebondie
De tes prés, copieuse et forte Normandie ?...
Ah! je ne guérirai jamais de mon pays!
N'est-il pas la douceur des feuillages cueillis
Dans la fraîcheur, la paix et toute l'innocence ?
Et qui donc a jamais guéri de son enfance ?...

First published in "Ferveur" by Lucie Delarue-Mardrus
(Paris : Editions De La Revue Blanche, 1902)

ELSA LASKER-SCHÜLER
GERMANY

Born 11th February 1869,
Wuppertal, Germany

Died 22nd January 1945,
Jerusalem, Palestine

Elsa was born in Elberfeld, which is now a suburb of Wuppertal in Germany but before the creation of the modern German state was then part of the North Rhine Confederation. Her parents were Jeanettte and Aaron Schueler – her father was a banker.

She married Jonathan Berthold Lasker - a doctor - in 1894 and moved with him to Berlin, where she studied art. Elsa's first full volume of poems was published in 1902, although she had various poems published individually before then.

Elsa divorced Lasker and married Georg Lewin, a writer, in 1903. Elsa's work gained her the reputation of being the 'leading female representative of German expressionism'. and she stood at the centre of Berlin's early modern culture at the turn of the 20th century.

The "Moderns," as the influential members of Berlin's artist community were called, along with many young Jewish intellectuals, rebelled against the typical bourgeois conventions of the time.

She was widely criticised for her bohemian lifestyle and, in 1933, moved to Switzerland to escape persecution by he Nazis. She travelled on to Palestine and in 1937 went to live in Jerusalem, where she died in 1945.

Als Der Blaue Reiter War Gefallen ...
(trans: As The Blue Rider Died...)

Griffen unsere Hände sich wie Ringe;-
Küßten uns wie Brüder auf den Mund.

Harfen wurden unsere Augen,
Als sie weinten: Himmlisches Konzert.

Nun sind unsere Herzen Waisenengel.
Seine tiefgekränkte Gottheit
Ist erloschen in dem Bilde: Tierschicksale.

A comment upon the death of German impressionist painter and printmaker Franz Marc of the expressionist "Blaue Reiter" artists group who was killed in France in March 1916.

Published in "Neue Jugend" magazine, Vol 1 Issue 11/12, Feb/Mar 1917, Page 245

Abschied (trans: Leaving)

Aber du kamst nie mit dem Abend-
ich saß im Sternenmantel.
...Wenn es an mein Haus pochte,
war es mein eigenes Herz.
Das hängt nun an jedem Türpfosten,
auch an deiner Tür;
zwischen Farren verlöschende Feuerrose
im Braun der Guirlande.
Ich färbte dir den Himmel brombeer
mit meinem Herzblut.
Aber du kamst nie mit dem Abend-
...Ich stand in goldenen Schuhen.

Published in "Die Kuppel (Die Gedichte - Zweiter Teil)" by Elsa Lasker-Schüler (Berlin: Verlag Paul Cassirer, 1920)

Mein Stilles Lied (trans: My Silent Song)

Mein Herz ist eine traurige Zeit,
Die tonlos tickt.
Meine Mutter hatte goldene Flügel,
Die keine Welt fanden.

Horcht, mich sucht meine Mutter,
Lichte sind ihre Finger und ihre Füße wandernde Träume.
Und süße Wetter mit blauen Wehen
Wärmen meine Schlummer

Immer in den Nächten,
Deren Tage meiner Mutter Krone tragen.
Und ich trinke aus dem Monde stillen Wein,
Wenn die Nacht einsam kommt.

Meine Lieder trugen des Sommers Bläue
Und kehrten düster heim.
– Ihr verhöhntet meine Lippe
Und redet mit ihr. –

Doch ich griff nach euren Händen,
Denn meine Liebe ist ein Kind und wollte spielen.

Und ich artete mich nach euch,
Weil ich mich nach dem Menschen sehnte.
Arm bin ich geworden
An eurer bettelnden Wohltat.
Und das Meer wird es wehklagen Gott.

Ich bin der Hieroglyph,
Der unter der Schöpfung steht
Und mein Auge ist der Gipfel der Zeit;
Sein Leuchten küßt Gottes Saum.

First published in "Der Siebente Tag" by Elsa Lasker Schüler (Berlin: Verlag des Vereins fur Kunst, Amelang-sche Buchhandung, 1905)

ADA NEGRI
ITALY

Born 3rd February 1870
Lodi, Italy

Died 11th January 1945
Milan, Italy

Ada was born on 3rd February 1870 to Giuseppe Negri and Vittoria Cornalba. She trained as a primary school teacher and taught at a school in Matta Viscanti on the Ticino River. Her first volume of poetry was published in 1892.

In March 1896 Ada married Giovanni Garlanda from Biella who fell in love with her through reading her poetry. In 1913 Ada separated from her husband and went to live in Switzerland, where she died on 11th January 1945.

The American actress Pola Negri adopted the name because she admired the poet.

Freschezza (trans: Freshness)

La tua freschezza, o creatura, è simile
al brusir della pioggia sulle foglie
di giugno, quando scoppian le magnolie
carnee sul ramo, e i gigli sembran calici

pieni d'acqua; o al crosciare della pioggia
d'autunno, quando l'olea-fràgrans pènetra
del suo profondo aroma anche le gocciole
lucenti, e chi il respira ha la vertigine;

o al sùbito mutar di luci e d'ombre
se passino le nuvole di marzo
con repentine acquate, e sprazzi vividi
di sol fra pianto e pianto, e un turbinìo
di pòllini nell'impeto del vento.

Parole Non Dette (trans: Unspoken Words)

Parole che la bocca mai non disse,
per pietà, per orgoglio o per paura,
che ai labbri spinse una demenza oscura,
che un più forte volere ivi confisse:

parole non di suono ma di palpito,
miste al sangue pulsante, alla saliva
di che il tacer s'abbevera, alla viva
carne che soffre, al cuor che batte a scalpito:

han, nel profondo ove s'accolgon bieche,
(e chi dir non le volle in sè le udrà
sempre) un'allucinante fissità
di facce spente, di pupille cieche.

O creatura dalle chiuse labbra,
sulla parte di te che fu soppressa
il tuo silenzio è pari a una compressa
gelida su ferita che si slabbra.

O creatura che disìo non chiama
più, che amor più non sveglia!... Un'ora sola
a te segnava Iddio per la parola
che non dicesti: ed or dentro ti clama.

Rannìcchiati in disparte, ingoia il pianto,
avvilùppati d'ombra. È tardi adesso
per la tua verità. Tu sei già presso
la soglia eterna, ove il silenzio è santo.

Ada Negri

Both poems first published in "Esilio" by Ada Negri.
(Milan: Editori Fratelli Treves, 1914)

AMALIA GUGLIELMINETTI
ITALY

Born 4th April 1881
Turin, Italy

Died 4th December 1941
Turin, Italy

Amalia was born in Turin to a middle class family, her father was Pietro Guglielminetti and her mother, Felicita Lavezzata. After the death of her father, the family went to live with her grandfather, who brought her up as a strict Catholic and sent her to be educated in a convent school.

She began writing poetry in 1901 for the "Gazetta del Popolo" newspaper, her poetry being published in their Sunday supplement. Amalia's first volume of poems was published in 1903, followed by volumes in 1908, 1917 and 1925.   Between 1916 and 1925 wrote books for children.

Amalia travelled throughout Italy lecturing and urging women to "speak out for themselves". She also supported fellow women writers. She began and edited a literary magazine – "La Seduzioni" (Seductions). In her own words, "to found a literary review is, for a woman, a more momentous event than that of taking a husband".

She died in 1941 in Turin following a fall during an air raid.

Il Desiderio (trans: Desire)

Il desiderio è taciturno. Saggio
sembra, ma in fondo alle pupille cova
la vïolenza del suo cuor selvaggio.

L'amore è sorda lotta, è dura prova
per chi assai l'ama, e a molti impeti sciocchi
avventa chi ben cerca e male trova.

Questo imparò colei che smarrì gli occhi
dietro i suoi sogni e ride ora, ma batte
le ciglia perché il pianto non trabocchi.

Poiché, se alcun le sue treccie ha disfatte,
od impresse d'un morso la sua gola,
o lasciò le sue labbra più scarlatte,
ella è pur sempre quella che va sola.

Amalia Guglieminetti

First published in "I Seduzioni" by Amalia Guglielminetti
(Turin : Editori S Lattes & C Librai, 1909)

AKIKO YOSANO

JAPAN

*Born 7th December 1878,
Osaka, Japan*

*Died 29th May 1942
Tokyo, Japan*

Pen name of Yosano Shiyo

Akiko Yosano was the pen-name of the Japanese writer, poet, feminist, pacifist and social reformer Sho Ho, who was born on 7th December 1878 in Sakai near Osaka to a wealthy family. Her father realised his daughter's intelligence and allowed her to have a good education. By the time she was eleven years old, Akiko was in charge of the family business making and selling Japanese sweets.

She began writing poetry as a teenager and in 1901, married Tekan Yosano, who edited the poetry magazine "Myojo" (Bright Star) a publication in which many of Akiko's poems were printed. She also had her first volume of poems published in 1901.

Akiko wrote a tremendous number of poems and essays and worked tirelessly for the cause of women's education, helping to found a school for girls - the Bunka Gaguin. She could, apparently, write as many as 50 poems in one session and, during the course of her lieftime, wrote somewhere between 20000 to 50000 poems, as well as 11 books of prose.

She gave burth to 13 children - 11 of whom survived to adulthood – and one of her grandchildren, Kaonu Yosano, is a leading Japanese politician.

Akiko Yosano died at the age of 63 on 29th May 1942 and is buried on the outskirts of Tokyo.

Thou Shalt Not Die

O my young brother, I cry for you
Don't you understand you must not die!
You who were born the last of all
Command a special store of parents' love
Would parents place a blade in children's hands
Teaching them to murder other men

Teaching them to kill and then to die?
Have you so learned and grown to twenty-four?

O my brother, you must not die!
Could it be the Emperor His Grace
Exposeth not to jeopardy of war
But urgeth men to spilling human blood
And dying in the way of wild beasts,
Calling such death the path to glory?
If His Grace possesseth noble heart
What must be the thoughts that linger there?

The poem was "Thou Shalt Not Die" written in 1904 and dedicated to her brother during the Russo-Japanese War. It was published in Myojo magazine and then set to music and became a protest song.

Black Hair

Black hair
Tangled in a thousand strands.
Tangled my hair and
Tangled my tangled memories
Of our long nights of love making

First published in "Midaregami" (Tangled Hair) by Akiko Yosano published in 1901[

AGNITA FEIS
NETHERLANDS

*Born 1881, Rotterdam,
Netherlands*

Died 1944

*Image: Portrait of Agnita Feis reading the Bible by
Theo van Doesburg 1907*

Agnita Henrica Feis was born in Rotterdam. Her father, Reiner Feis, was a textile merchant. The family moved to The Hague, where Angnita's Father died in 1886. Agnita and her mother (Antje Sijnes Hoijtema) then moved to Apeldoorn.

In 1903, Agnita met the artist Theo Van Doesburg. They married in May 1910 and moved to Amsterdam. It is Theo Van Doesburg's painting of his wife reading the bible (image above) that illustrates this biography. Agnita continued to write and paint, keeping her own name; her work was published regularly in the Dutch journal "Unit" (De Stijl), edited by the couple's friend Anthony Cook, the Dutch writer and poet.

The Netherlands were neutral during WW1 but nevertheless after the incident at Sarajevo they mobilised their army and Agnita Feis's husband was based near the Belgian border.

In 1914, Van Doesburg was mobilised and the marriage began to go wrong. Towards the end of 1915, Agnita published a volume of her own poems entitled "War. Verses in Stacatto" and, in spite of their marriage problems, Van Doesburg designed the front cover of her book.

Feis and Van Doesburg were divorced on 11th May 1917 and Feis was very bitter. Very little is known about her later life. She died in 1944.

De Koning Rijdt
(trans: The King Rides)

Hij rijdt te paard,
Hij rijdt langs 't woud.
Hij kijkt omhoog.
Hij ziet lechts goud.

Hij rijdt in goud.
Hij rijdt te paard.
Hij ziet niet wat
er ligt op d'aard!

Hij rijdt. Hij rijdt!
Hij schertst! Hij lacht.
Zijn ziel is steeds
zoo goed, zoo zacht.

Hij rijdt in goud,
Hij rijdt in zon.
Hij's blij. Er was
een slag: Hij won.

Hij blinkt van licht.
Hij's goed die vorst.
Hij ziet toch niet
die korst? Die korst

van bloed? Van bloed!
Van bloed! Van bloed!

Van bloed in 't bosch!
Van bloed op 't land?
Van bloed op kleed
en op zijn hand?

Het paard ruikt bloed,
Het paard staat stil,
Maar 't paard heeft toch
geen eigen wil?

Hij rijdt te paard.
Hij rijdt langs 't woud.
Hij rijdt. Hij rijdt!
Hij rijdt in goud!!

Menschenmateriaal
(trans: Human Material)

Het is maar bloed.
Het is maar been.

Is 't heusch maar stof?
Is 't stof alleen?

Men schendt natuur.
Men schendt den geest.

Men is geen mensch.
Men is geen beest!

Werp maar den mensch
in 't vuur! Ga voort!

Maar 't is ùw ziel,
die wordt vermoord!

Both poems originally published in "Oorloog. Verzen in Staccato" by Agnita Feis.
Self Published 1915

MARIA PAWLIKOWSKA – JASNORZEWSKA
Poland

Born 24th November 1891
Krakow, Congress Poland

Died 9th July 1945
Manchester, England

During the First World War Poland did not exist as the country we know in the 21st Century – its modern day territories had been divided up as part of the Russian, Austro-Hungarian and Prussian (later German) Empires in 1815.

At the time that Maria was born, Krakow was part of Congress Poland which was a semi-autonomous territory under Russian control,

Maria was a poet, playwright and painter, known as the "queen of lyrical poetry" and "Poland's Sappho".

She was born Maria Kossak into a family of noble origin. Both her parents were renowned, respected artists who painted military subjects. Maria was educated privately at home and studied English, French and German, becoming fluent in all three languages. She painted and wrote poetry from an early age.

In 1915, Maria married Wladyslaw Bzowski, an officer in the Austrian Army but the marriage did not last long and was annulled.

In 1919, Maria married Jan Pawlikowski, a writer, after which her literary career began in earnest. Her first volume of poetry – "Blue Almonds" - was published in 1922. By 1929 that marriage had also failed and was annulled.

In 1924, Maria began writing plays and published her second volume of poetry – "Pink Magic" which she also illustrated herself. In 1931 she married Stefan Jasnorzewski, an officer in the Polish Air Force. Maria was awarded the Golden Laurel of the Polish Academy of Literature in 1935 and the Cracow Literary Prize in 1937.

The couple moved to England at the beginning of the Second World War settling in Blackpool. Maria became seriously ill, had two operations in hospital in Manchester and died on 9th July 1945. She is buried in a cemetery in Manchester and the headstone was funded by the Union of Polish Writers Abroad.

Sen (trans: Sleep)

Iść przez sen ku tobie,
w twe słodkie ręce obie...
przez pola długie ogromnie,
sadzone w rzędy doniczek...
samych niebieskich konwalii
i szafirowych goryczek...
...przejść przez jezioro nieduże,
zrobione z drewnianej balii...
i trochę nieprzytomnie
iść dalej przez bór ciemny, w którym kwitną róże,
lecz w którym się nie pali ani jedna świeca...
gdzie straszy stary niedźwiedź dziecinny zza pieca,
dziś przerobiony na kota...
I widzieć w oddali już twoją psią budę
z kryształu, blachy i złota...
przedrzeć się z trudem poprzez dziwną grudę...
i jeszcze ten rów przebyć...
- potknąć się - i już nie być.

*First published in "Niebieskie Migdały" by Maria Kossakow Pawlikowska
(Krakow: Spolki Wydawniczej, 1922)*

FLORBELA ESPANÇA
Portugal

Born 8th December 1894
Vila Viçosa, Portugal

Died 8th December 1930
Matosinhos, Portugal

Florbela Espança was born Flor Bela Lobo to single mother Antonia da Conceição Lobo in 1894 at Vila Viçosa, birthplace of Catherine of Braganza and home estate of the royal family of Portugal and Brazil.

After the death of her mother in 1908, she was brought up by her Mother's employers Maria and Joao-Maria Espança and took their family name. She began writing poetry at a very early age and was, in fact, one of the first Portuguese women to attend secondary school. At that time, it was very unusual for women in Portugal to be highly educated.

By the time of her first marriage in 1915, she had already had poems published in local newspapers. She graduated from university with a degree in literature in 1917 and became the first woman to enrol in the law school at the University of Lisbon.

It seems that Florbela had a turbulent life for she married three times, divorcing twice. She died on 8th December 1930 on her 36th birthday, leaving a legacy of many novels, poems and short stories.

Many of her poems have been put to music and in the 1980s the words of "Perdidamente" (trans; Madly) were used a pop song that was a massive hit, which meant that a whole new generation came to learn about Florbela.

Her life was recently dramatised in a 3-part special on Portuguese television called "Perdidamente Florbela".

Lagrimas Ocultas (trans: Hidden Tears)

Se me ponho a scismar em outras éras
Em que ri e cantei, em que era qu'rida,
Parece-me que foi noutras esféras,
Parece-me que foi numa outra vida...

E a minha triste bôca dolorida
Que dantes tinha o rir das primavéras,
Esbate as linhas graves e severas
E cae num abandôno de esquecida!

E fico, pensativa, olhando o vago...
Toma a brandura plácida dum lago
O meu rôsto de monja de marfim...

E as lágrimas que choro, branca e calma,
Ninguem as vê brotar dentro da alma!
Ninguem as vê cair dentro de mim!

Languidez (trans: Listlessness)

Fecho as pálpebras roxas, quase pretas,
Que poisam sobre duas violetas,
Asas leves cansadas de voar...

E a minha boca tem uns beijos mudos...
E as minhas mãos, uns pálidos veludos,
Traçam gestos de sonho pelo ar...

*Both poems first published in "Livro De Magoas" by Florbela Espanca
(Lisbon: Tipografia Mauricio, 1919)*

ELENA VACARESCU
Rumania

Born 21ˢᵗ September 1864
Bucharest, Rumania

Died 17ᵗʰ February 1947
Paris, France

Also known as Helene Vacaresco

Romania was part of the Ottoman Empire but after the Russo-Turkish War of 1877 – 1878 declared independence and joined Russia.

Elena or Héléne Vacarescu was born on 21st September 1864 in Bucharest to an aristocratic family. She was educated by an English governess – a Miss Allen - and went on to study French in Paris.

Elena met Elizabeth of Wied, who was Queen of Romania at the time as the wife of King Carol I of Romania, and became one of her ladies in waiting. Elizabeth was also a poet.

Following an affair with the heir to the Romanian throne where the Constitution forbade the marriage of the heir to the throne to a Romanian, Elena was sent to live in Paris.

She was a delegate to the League of Nations 1925 – 1926 and a delegate of the Paris Peace Conference at the end of World War 2.

Elena died in Paris on 17th February 1947.

Le Jardin Passionné (trans: The Passionate Garden)

Il a fallu mettre des pierres
Autour du sang qui la remplit,
Et que l'odeur des sapinières
Ne vienne pas jusqu'à son lit.

Doigts qui savez comment on brise
Et comment on déchire, ô doigts
Qui touchez sans deuil ni surprise
L'air vide des anciennes voix.

Doigts pour qui l'azur et la cendre
Sont un même et futile jeu,
Ah ! vous auriez mieux fait d'étendre
Sa flamme en un linceul de feu.

Les pierres s'écrasent sur elle.
Et tous les jours vont lui disant :
« Celui que ton désir appelle
D'un éternel soulèvement ;

« Celui qui, sous les sapinières,
Pressait ton sein passionné,
N'ose point déranger les pierres
Du tombeau sûr qu'il t'a donné. »

First published in "Le Jardin Passioné" by Helene Vacaresco
(Paris: Plon-Nourrit et Cie, 1908)

Note:
The Royal Families and nobilities of numerous European countries wrote and spoke in French during this period and it is quite rare to find literature written in the indiginous tongue of some of these countries. This is why this Rumanian poet has written in French. The search, however, will continue in later volumes of this ongoing project....

ANNA AKMATOVA
RUSSIA

Born 23rd June 1889,
Odessa, Ukraine

Died 5th May 1966,
Leningrad, Soviet Union

Anna Akmatova was the pen name of Andreyevna Gorenko. She was a prolific, internationally acclaimed poet but her work was condemned during Stalin's rule. However, she chose to remain in Russia in order to take note of what was happening.

Anna was born in Bolshoy Fontan near Odessa on the Black Sea. Her father was a naval engineer and her mother, Inna Stagova - they were descended from Russian nobility and Anna's grandfather Erasm Ivanovich Stogov was related to the poet Anna Banina.The family moved to Tsarskoye Selo near St. Petersburg before Anna was a year old.

She began writing poetry when she was eleven. Anna studied law at Kiev University, then went to study literature in St. Petersburg. She met Nokolay Gumilev also a poet in 1903 and he encouraged her writing, publishing some of her poems in his publication "Sirius". The couple married in Kiev in 1910 and honeymooned in Paris, where Anna met Modigliani, who painted her several times.

Anna soon became a very popular and acclaimed poet. The First World War and the 1917 Revolution in Russia had a profound affect on Anna's style. In 1918, she divorced Gumilev and married Vladimir Shilejko. In 1921 Gumilev was arrested and shot. Anna's work was banned in 1925, however she continued to write. The regime was very hard on intellectuals and many of Anna's friends were deported to the Gulags.

Anna married her lifelong friend Nikolai Punin, who was repeatedly arrested and eventually died in the Gulag in 1953. During the Second World War, Anna read poetry to soldiers at the front. Her son was also frequently arrested and was sentenced to ten years in Siberia in 1949.

During the final years of her life, Anna lived with the Punin family in Leningrad (now renamed St Petersburg). Robert Frost visited her in 1962 and in 1965 she was permitted to travel to Italy and England in order to receive the Taormina Prize and an honorary degree from Oxford University. She died in the spring of 1966, leaving a vast legacy of work.

My Voice Is Weak, But Not My Will

My voice is weak but not my will,
It's better even without love.
High skies and mountain winds,
And my thoughts now innocent.

Insomnia, my nurse, is elsewhere.
I'm not brooding by cold ashes.
And the curved hand on the tower clock,
Is no longer a deadly arrow.

How the past loses power over the heart!
Freedom is near. Everything's simple,
See how the sunlight falls across
The wet ivy this spring.

First published in Belaya Staya (White Flock) by Anna Akhmativa in 2000 copies. (Petrograd: Hyperborea, 1917)

Petrograd, 1919

Caged in this savage capital,
We have forgotten forever
The townships, the lakes, the steppes,
The dawns, of our great motherland.
In the circuit of blood-stained days and nights,
A bitter languor overcomes us...
No one wishes to come to our aid,
Because we choose to remain here,
Because, in love with our city,
More than the wings of liberty,
We preserved to ourselves,
Its palaces, flames, and waters.
Now another time draws near,
The wind of death chills the heart,
And Peter's sacred city,
Will be our unsought monument.

Everything's Looted, Betrayed and Traded

Everything's looted, betrayed and traded,
Black death's wing's overhead.
Everything's eaten by hunger, un-sated,
So why does a light shine ahead?

By day, a mysterious wood, near the town,
Breathes out cherry, a cherry perfume.
By night, on July's sky, deep, and transparent,
New constellations are thrown.

And something miraculous will come
Close to the darkness and ruin,
Something no-one, no-one, has known,
Though we've longed for it since we were children.

Both poems originally published in "Anno Domini MCMXXI" by Anna Akhmatova,
Published in Petrograd in 1922

JELENA
SPIRIDONOVIC-SAVIC
SERBIA

*Born 11th January 1891
Sabac, Serbia*

*Died September 1974
Belgrade, Yugoslavia*

Jelena was born on 1th January 1891 into a family of doctors –
Father Michael and Mother Olga Spiridonovic.

She studied in Trieste before the First World War and travelled to
New York, Milan and Vienna to study philosophy.

Jelena married Vladislav Savic, Consul General of Yugoslavia, who
was also a poet and writer and who started the Socialist Party of
Serbia in 1903.

Jelena, who published her first volume of poetry in 1926, was a
member of the Pen Club and the Society of Writers of Serbia.

She died in Belgrade in September 1974.   Much of Jelena's work
from 1941 until 1954 remains unpublished.

Sunce (trans: Sun)

I ponesi me,
ponesi tako, u sjajnom
dugom putu
tvoga zlaćanog zraka,
o, Sunce,
Svetlosti moćne
vodi me
iz Carstva mraka.

Jelena Spiridonovic-Savic

First published in "Sa Uskih Staza" (From The Narrow Paths) by Jelena Spiridonovic-Savic. (Belgrade: Izdanje SB Cvijanovica, 1919)

Pergamente (trans: Parchments)

No jednog dana kroz vekova osam,
ja narode vidim, međ njima Britone,
plavi, isti takvi kao i ja što sam,
dolaze da dele s vama čase bone...

najbolju će decu britanskih sinova
progutati bliskog Helesponta vali
Tvom narodu Život počeće tad s nova,
vaskrsnuće opet stari Ideali.

Jelena Spiridonovic-Savic

First published in "Pergamente" by Jelena Spiridonovic-Savic. (Belgrade: Izdanje SB Cvijanovica, 1923)

APPENDIX: FULL LIST OF POETS SO FAR (JULY 2013)...

This is a list of all of the poets that I have found do far and it is my hope to – eventually - cover them all in future volumes of Female Poets Of The First World War.

Please note that these are not necessarily "war poets" as such and in order to qualify for inclusion on this list, they only need to have been alive and actively writing during the period of the Great War.

As such, many of the poems that I am citing are not about the war at all, merely written then and some of the poems were not necessarily written during the war at all but beforehand or afterwards.

As my research has progressed, it has become very clear that there were far more women who wrote poetry during the 1914 - 1918 period than the few mentioned in many of the anthologies compiled so far. I feel strongly that their voices deserve to be heard.

BRITISH

A
Margot Robert ADAMSON
Georgette AGNEW
Marian ALLEN
Jessie Annie ANDERSON (b. 1861 - Scottish
Lilian M. ANDERSON
Marion ANGUS (1866 - 1946) - Scottish

B
Enid BAGNOLD (27th October 1889 - 31st March 1981) (Nurse then driver in France)
Rachel BATES (Wirral) – SEE PAGE 45 OF THIS VOLUME
Dorothy Julie BAYNES
Mary BEAZLEY
Madeline Ida BEDFORD
Janet BEGBIE
Maud Anna BELL (Serbian Relief Fund)
Frances BELLERBY (1899 – 1975)
Stella BENSON (1892 - 1933) – SEE PAGE 8 OF THIS VOLUME
Matilda BETHAM-EDWARDS
Nora BOMFORD
Mary BOOTH
Lilian BOWES LYON (1895 - 1949)
Mary Elizabeth BOYLE (brother killed in opening days of the War)
Catherine BRIDSON (Wirral) – SEE PAGE 48 OF THIS VOLUME
Beatrix BRICE MILLER
Sybil BRISTOWE (brother killed early 1917)
Vera BRITTAIN (1896 - 1970) (Nurse - VAD - Brother killed in Italy)
Alice Mary BUCKTON (1867 - 1944) (Emigrated to South Africa)

C.A.L.T.
May WEDDERBURN-CANNAN (1893 - 1973) (VAD + Intelligence Service; engaged to Bevil Quiller-Couch)
Elizabeth CHANDLER FORMAN
Mary G. CHERRY
Frances A. CHESTERTON (1869 - 1938)

Mary CHOLMONDELEY (niece of Stella Benson) (8.6.1859 – 15.07.1925) (worked as a clerk in Carlton House Terrace Hospital)
Agatha CHRISTIE (nee Miller) (1890 – 1976 VAD Torquay) – SEE PAGE 10 THIS VOLUME
Isabel C. CLARKE (born Plymouth)
Alice E. COLLINGE (1869 – 1960)
Mary Gabrielle COLLINS
Frances CORNFORD (1886 – 1960)
Margaret CROPPER
Nancy CUNARD (1896 - 1965)

D
Elizabeth DARYUSH (Daughter of Robert Bridges) (1887 - 1976)
Helena DEREZINSKA (Lancashire)
Helen DIRCKS
Eva DOBELL (1867 - 1963) (Niece of poet Sydney Dobell) (Nurse)
Sarah DOUDNEY (1841 - 1926)
O. DOUGLAS (Pen name of Anna Masterfar BUCHAN - John Buchan's sister)
Agnes E. DREY (Lancashire)

E
Helen Parry EDEN (1885 -

F
Agnes FALCONER
Eleanor FARJEON (London; 1881 - 1965)
V. Helen FRIEDLAENDER

G
Lilian GARD
Alexandra Ethelreda GRANTHAM (eldest son killed WW1)
Nora GRIFFITHS
I. GRINDLEY (Queen Mary's Army Auxilliary Corps)
Diana GURNEY
Dorothy Frances GURNEY (1858 - 1932)

H
Cicely HAMILTON (1872 - 1952) (organised nursing care; joined Army Aux. entertained troops)
Helen HAMILTON
Isabel WESTCOTT HARPER
Ada May HARRISON
Agnes CROZIER HERBERTSON
May HERSHEL-CLARKE
Ethel M. HEWITT
Constance HOLLAR
Winifred HOLTBY (Nursed in France) – SEE PAGE 13 OF THIS VOLUME
Theresa HOOLEY
Violet HUNT
Isobel W. HUTCHISON
Mildred HUXLEY

J
Catherine M. JACKSON (Wirral) – SEE PAGE 49 OF THIS VOLUME
Violet JACOB (1863 - 1947 Born Violet Kennedy-Erskine in Scotland m. Major Arthur Jacob of 20th Hussars - son killed on the Somme 1916)
Storm JAMESON
Elinor JENKINS (1893 - 1920)

K
Edith A. KAHIA (Lancashire)

Anna GORDON KEOWN
Annie L. KNOWLES (Lancashire)

L
Margery LAWRENCE
Winifred M. LETTS (1882 - 1972) – SEE PAGE 16 OF THIS VOLUME
Olive E. LINDS
Geraldine E. LYSTER (Lancashire)

M
Irene Rutherford McLEOD
Dame Rose MACAULAY (1881 - 1958) (Descendent of Lord Macaulay)
Helen MACKAY (1891 - 1965)
Nina MACDONALD
Miss Isobel MARCHBANK
Nina MARDEL (VAD)
Alice MAUD
Charlotte MEW
Alice MEYNELL (1847 - 1922)
Olga MILLER (nee KATZIN) 1896 -
Sophie MILLER
Frances Evelyn MILLETT
Miss G.M. MITCHELL
Lady Gertrude MOBERLEY (1860 -

N
Edith NESBIT (1858 - 1924) (m. BLAND)
Eileen NEWTON
The Honourable Eleanour NORTON (1881 -)

O
Moira O'NEILL (1864 - 1955)
Carola OMAN (1897 - 1978) Nurse with Red + Western Front 1916 - 1919 m. Sir Geralde
Lenanton
Emily ORR
Florence OVERTON (Lancashire)

P
Margaret PETERSON (1883 - 1933. Pen name: Glint Green)
Ruth PITTER (7 November 1897 - 29 February 1992) (Worked at the War Office 1915 - 1917
Jessie POPE (18.3.1868 - 14.12.1941 - b, Leicester m. Babington Lenton
Dame Margaret POSTGATE COLE (1893 - 1980)
Irene R. POTTER
Mary PRALL
Marjorie PRATT
Louise PRIOR

Q
Inez QUILTER

R
Dollie RADFORD (nee Maitland) (1858 – 1920)
Dorothy Una RATCLIFFE (1887 - 1967 b. Yorkshire)
Constance Ada RENSHAW (Sheffield. 1891 - 1964)
Dorothy RICHARDSON (b. Abingdon 17th May 1873 - d. Beckenham 17th June 1957. m. Alan
Odle 1917)
Ursula ROBERTS (1887 - 1975) (b. India; educated Highgate and London University) Pen name
Susan MILES)
Margaret E. ROWNTREE (nee Fish m. 1926) (Born Fleetwood 1899 - 1983) – SEE PAGE 20

S
Lady Margaret SACKVILLE
Vita SACKVILLE-WEST (1892 - 1962)
Dorothy L. SAYERS
Ethel SCHEFFAUER
Lady Aimee BYNG SCOTT (1868 - 1953)
Edith HOPE-SCOTT (Lancashire)
Fredegond SHOVE (nee MAITLAND) (1889 – 1949) – SEE PAGE 23 OF THIS VOLUME
May SINCLAIR (born Rock Ferry, Wirral 1865 - 1946) Nurse in France 1914 – SEE PAGE 25
Edith SITWELL (born Scarborough 1887 - 1964) – SEE PAGE 29
Cicely FOX SMITH (Born Lymm, Cheshire; educated Manchester) – SEE PAGE 32
Stevie SMITH (1902 - 1971) "Not waving but drowning"
Freya STARK (1893 - 1993)
Dorothy Margaret STEWART
Suzanne STONE
Marie Carmichael STOPES (1880 - 1954) (First female science lecturer at Manchester University)
Muriel STUART (- 1967) (Founded P.E.N. Club in 1921)
Millicent SUTHERLAND ((1867 - 1955)(Milicent Gower, Duchess of Sutherland) (Nurse in France.
Painted by Victor Tardieu) – SEE PAGE 35 OF THIS VOLUME
Mary SYMON (Scottish)

T
Emily HOWSON TAYLOR (1879 -
Gwen TAYLOR
Rachel Annand TAYLOR (1876 - 1960)
Ruth TAYLOR
Judith BRUNDRETT-TWESDALE
Joan THOMPSON (With the Red Cross to France)
Aelfrida TILLYARD (1883 -
Iris TREE (1897 - 1968) (Bloomsbury Group - friend of Nancy Cunard)
Alys FANE TROTTER (1863 - 1962) lived in South Africa during 1890s
Ada TYRELL

U/V
Evelyn UNDERHILL   (worked with SSAFA and Naval Intelligence)
Alberta VICKRIDGE (b. Bradford, Educated Bradford Girls' Grammar. VAD nurse)
Viviane VERNE

W
Sylvia TOWNSEND WARNER (1893 -) Worked in Munitions Factory
Mary WEBB (1881 - 1927 b. Leighton, nr. Wrekin, Shropshire; educated Southport)
Mary Morison WEBSTER
M. Winifred WEDGWOOD (VAD)
Dorothy WELLESLEY (1889 - 1956)
Catherine DURNING WHETHAM (Devon)
Lucy WHITMELL
Anna WICKHAM (1884 - 1947)
Carolyn Crosby WILSON
Marjorie WILSON
Margaret L. WOODS
Elizabeth WORDSWORTH (1840 - 1932)

AMERICAN
Zoe AKINS (1886 - 1958)
Margaret Steele ANDERSON (1867 - 1921)

Karle Wilson BAKER (1878 - 1960)
Djuna BARNES (1892 - 1982)

111

Natalie Clifford BARNEY (1876 - 1972; lived in Paris for over 60 years)
Pauline BARRINGTON (1876 -
Katharine Lee BATES (12.081859 - 28.03.1929: "America the Beautiful")
Louise BOGAN (1897 - 1970)
Mary BORDEN (lived in England. Mobile hospital in France)
Amelia Josephine BURR (1878 - 1968)

Nancy CAMPBELL
Grace ELLERHY CHANNING (1862 - 1937; France and Italy as a War Correspondent)
Florence van Leer Earle Nicholson COATES (1850 - 1927)
Helen Gray CONE (1859 - 1934)
Grace Hazard CONKLING (1878 - 1958)
Adelaide CRAPSEY
Charlotte Holmes CRAWFORD

Olive TILFORD DARGAN
Mary Carolyn DAVIES
Hilda Dolittle or H.D. (1886 - 1961)
Vita DUTTON-SCUDDER (1861 - 1954)

Gabrielle ELLIOTT (American Fund for French Wounded; Nursing Committee for the Council of
National Defence)

S. Gertrude FORD
Lena GILBERT BROWN FORD – SEE PAGE 58 OF THIS VOLUME

Theodosia GARRISON
Charlotte Perkins GILMAN (1860 - 1935)
Muriel Elsie GRAHAM (1909 - 1987)
Louise Imogen GUINEY (1861 - 1920)

Mary M.J. HENDERSON (Lived in UK. Went to Russia and Serbia with Elsa Inglis)
Alice Corbin HENDERSON (1881 - 1949)
Katherine HOWARD

Amy LOWELL (1874 - 1925)

Florence RIPLEY MASTIN
Moina BELLE MICHAEL (The Poppy Lady) – SEE PAGE 51 OF THIS VOLUME
Ruth Comfort MITCHELL
Edna St. Vincent MILLAY
Harriet MONROE (Founded and edited "Poetry" the first American poetry magazine)
Marianne MOORE (1887 - 1972)
Aline MURRAY (1888 - 1941)

Grace Fallow NORTON (1876 - 1926)

Dorothy PARKER (1893 - 1967)
Marge PIERCY

Lizette WOODWORTH REESE (1856 - 1935)
Laura E. RICHARDS (1850 - 1943)
Edith Grenstead ROCHESTER
Edith RUTTER-LEATHAM

Vida Dutton SCUDDER (1861 - 1954)
Gertrude STEIN (1874 - 1946)
Charlotte PERKINS STETSON

Sarah TEASDALE
Lesbia THANET
Edith M. THOMAS (1854 - 1925)
Rose Hartwick THORPE (1850 - 1939)

Marie van VORST (Organised American Ambulance Corps; set up workshops in Rome)
Grace VANAMEE (1876 - 1946) – SEE PAGE 61 OF THIS VOLUME

Mrs G.O. WARREN
Edith WHARTON (1862 - 1937) (Paris WW1 - nursed)
Ella WHEELER WILCOX (1850 - 1919) (To the Western Front in 1918) – SEE PAGE 55 OF THIS
VOLUME
Margaret WIDDAMER
Margaret ADELAIDE WILSON

AUSTRIAN
*Ingeborg BACHMANN (1926 - 1973)
* Ingeborg is here because I am having trouble finding any Austrian First World War poets and by
kind permission and suggestion of Mike Lyons, who translated some of Ingeborg's poems.

AUSTRO-HUNGARIAN
Rose AUSLANDER (11.05.1901 – 03.01.1988)

AUSTRALIAN
Emily BULCOCK (1877 - 1969) – SEE PAGE 68 OF THIS VOLUME
Ada CAMBRIDGE A.C. (1844 - 1926)
Violet B. CRAMER
Zora CROSS (1890 - 1964)
Edith May ENGLAND (1899 - 1979)
Nellie EVANS (1883 - 1944)
May Hannay FOOT (1846 - 1918)
Mary Elizabeth FULLERTON (1868 - 1946)
Dame Mary GILMORE (1965 - 1962)
Lesbia HARFORD (1891 - 1927)
Winsome JENNINGS
Alice GORE JONES (1887 - 1961) – SEE PAGE 66 OF THIS VOLUME
Marion KNOWLES
Dorothea McKELLAR
Nina MURDOCK (1890 - 1976)
Agnes ROSE-SOLEY
Ethel TURNER (1872 - 1958 - born Doncaster, England)
Elizabeth von AMIN (1866 - 1941)

BELGIAN
Marie NIZET – SEE PAGE 74 OF THIS VOLUME
Alice NAHON (1896 - 1938)

BRAZILIAN
Brazil declared war on Germany on 26th October 1917
Cora Coralina (20 August 1889 – 10 April 1985)
Cecilia Meireles (7.11.1901 – 9.11.1964)
Adalgisa Nery (29.10.1905 – 7.6.1980)

BULGARIA
Bulgaria, which at that time was still recovering from the effects of previous wars, joined WW1 on the side of the Central Powers from 15th October 1915 when war was declared on Serbia until 30th September 1918 when the Armistice of Thessalonica was signed.
Elisaveta BAGRYANA (1893 - 1991)
Dora GABE (1886 - 1983)

CANADIAN
Jean BLEWETT (1872 - 1934) – SEE PAGE 63 OF THIS VOLUME
Helene Jane COLEMAN (1860 - 1953)
Marie JOUSSAYE (1864 - 1949)
Susan Frances HARRISON (1859 - 1935)
Norah M. HOLLAND (1876 - 1925)
Isabel MACKAY (Isabel Ecclestone - 1875 - 1928)
Lucy Maud MONTGOMERY (1874 - 1942)
Marjorie L.C. PICKTHALL (1883 - 1922)
Isabella WATSON (Poem about Edith Cavell)

CHILEAN
Chile helped the Allied cause by seizing the German-owned Nitrate and Copper mines
Gabriela MISTRAL (1889 - 1957 - pen name of Lucila Godoy Alcayaga) – SEE PAGE 77

CHINESE
China sent a large contingent of workers to help 'behind the scenes'. They also helped clear up the aftermath. Many of them died and they are commemorated in a special cemetery
Bing XIN – SEE PAGE 79 OF THIS VOLUME

DUTCH
Agnita FEIS – SEE PAGE 95 OF THIS VOLUME
Henriette ROLAND HOLST (1869 - 1952)
Augusta PEAUX (1859 - 1944)
Giza RITSCHL (1869 - 1942)
Nine van der SCHAAF (1882 - 1973)
Margo SHARTEN-ANTINK
Helene SWARTH (1859 - 1941)
Jacqueline van der WAALS (1868 - 1922)

FINNISH
Finland was part of the Russian Empire during the First World War and some of her soldiers served in the Russian Army until they declared independence on 6th December 1917.
Katri VALA (1901 - 1944)
Edith SÖDERGRAN (1892 - 1923) – SEE PAGE 82 OF THIS VOLUME

FRENCH
Marie DAUGUET (1860 - 1942)
Lise DEHARME (1898? - 1980)
Lucie DELARUE-MARDRUS (1874 - 1945- nurse in WW1) – SEE PAGE 84 OF THIS VOLUME
Marguerite DURAND (Editor of La Fronde)
Rosemonde GERARD (1886 - 1953)
Miriam HARRY (Maria Rosette SHAPIRA)
Gerard d'HOUVILLE (Nom de plume - 1875 - 1963)
Amelie MURAT (1882 - 1940)
Anna de NOAILLES (1876 - 1933)
Louisa PAULIN (1888 - 1944)
Cecile PERIN (1877 - 1959)
Cecile SAUVAGE (1883 - 1927)
Colette YVER (

GERMAN
Vicky BAUM
Anna BAHR-HILDENBERG
Isla FRANKE (1881 - 1938)
Claire GOLL (1890 - 1977)
Emily HENNINGS (1885 - 1948)
Elizabeth LANGASSER (1899 - 1950)
Berta LASK
Thekla LINGEN
Lya MARA
Elizabeth PAULSEN
Else LASKER SCHULER - SEE PAGE 86 OF THIS VOLUME

HEBREW
Rachel BLUWSTEIN (Rachel ISRAEL) (1890 - 1931)

INDIAN
Nalini Bala DEVI (1898 - 1977)
Sarojini NAIDU (1879 - 1949) – SEE PAGE 70 OF THIS VOLUME

IRISH
Jane BARLOW (1857 - 1917)
Eva GORE BOOTH
Elizabeth BOWEN (Downe House Pupil WW1) (1899 - 1973)
Kathleen KNOX
May O'ROURKE (Became Secretary to Thomas Hardy in 1923)
Dora SIGERSON SHORTER (1866 - 1918)
Katharine TYNAN (1861 - 1931)
Helen WADDELL

ITALIAN
Italy declared war on the Austro-Hungarian Empire on 23rd May 1915 and on Germany on 29th August 1916.
Elena CANINO (1898 - 1939)
Amalia GUGLIELMINETTI – SEE PAGE 91 OF THIS VOLUME
Ada NEGRI – SEE PAGE 89 OF THIS VOLUME

JAPANESE
Fukao SUMAKO (1893 - 1974)
Akiko YOSANO (1878 - 1942) – SEE PAGE 93 OF THIS VOLUME

NEW ZEALAND
Mary Ursula BETHELL (1874 - 19450
Eileen DUGGAN (1894 - 1972)
Katherine MANSFIELD (1888 - 1923)

POLISH
Maria PAWLIKOWSKA-JASNORZEWSKA (24.11.1891 Krakow – 09.07 1945 Manchester) – SEE PAGE 97 OF THIS VOLUME
Magdalena SAMOZWANIEL (1894 - 1972)

PORTUGUESE
Portugal is England's oldest ally - dating back to the time of John O'Gaunt whose daughter married the King of Portugal bringing tea and marmalade to England. Portugal sent troops, equipment and medical personnel to help the Allies during WW1
Fernanda de CASTRO
Florbela ESPANÇA – SEE PAGE 99 OF THIS VOLUME
Marta MESQUITA DE CAMARA
Virginia VITORINO

ROMANIAN

Romania had been part of the Ottoman Empire but after the Russo-Turkish War of 1877 - 1878, they declared independence and joined Russia

Izabela SADOVEANU-EVAN (24.02.1870 – 06.08.1941)
Elena VACARESCU (21.9.1864 Bucharest – 17.02.1947 Paris) – SEE PAGE 101
Elizabeth of WIED (1843 - 1916) (Married King Carol I of Roumania)

RUSSIAN

Anna AKHMATOVA (1889 -1966 from the Ukraine) – SEE PAGE 103 OF THIS VOLUME
Marina TSVETAEVA

SERBIAN

Jelena DIMITRIJEVIC (1862 - 1945)
Danica MARKOVIC (1879 - 1932)
Jelena SPIRIDONOVIC SAVIC (1890 – 1974) – SEE PAGE 106 OF THIS VOLUME

SOUTH AFRICAN

Edith L.M. KING (1871 - 1962) – SEE PAGE 72 OF THIS VOLUME

SWEDISH

Elsa BESKOW (1874 - 1953)

ALSO AVAILABLE FROM THE SAME PUBLISHER

If you have enjoyed this poetry booklet, why not have a look at our wider selection of publications embracing poetry, sports and other fascinating subjects. There are new additions to the range being added all the time, so do keep an eye on the website!

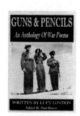

| **SELECTED POEMS 2012**
Over 50 Of The Best Entries From The 2012 Pendle War Poetry Competition
Edited by Paul Breeze
ISBN 978-0-9539782-7-4
74 pages paperback
Selling Price: £5.00 | **Purple Patches**
A collection of poems, songs and short stories from the fountain pen of Lucy London
ISBN: 978-1-909643-00-0
42 pages paperback
Selling Price £4.00 | **Guns & Pencils**
An Anthology Of War Poetry
By Lucy London
ISBN: 978-0-9539782-2-9
26 pages paperback
Selling Price: £4.00 | **Blackpool To Bond Street!**
The fascinating story of Amy Blackburn – pioneer of the makeover
By Joan Shaw
ISBN: 978-0-9539782-5-0
60 pages paperback
Selling Price: £6.00 |

Full details can be found at www.poshupnorth.com

PENDLE WAR POETRY COMPETITION

FREE TO ENTER

4 JUDGING CATEGORIES:
Local Pendle Adult
UK National Adult
Under 18
Overseas

In photo: Winner of 2012 Under 18 Category
Meredith Graham from Camberley in Surrey, with
Pendle MP Andrew Stephenson

For Details Of How To Enter, Full Competition
Rules & Prizes, See The Official Website at

www.pendlewarpoetry.com

Sponsored by:

ISAAC ROSENBERG (1890-1918)
£92.000 Appeal To Finance A Commemorative Statue

Isaac Rosenberg, one of the greatest of the First World War poets and a talented artist, has not received the widespread recognition he deserves.

The son of Jewish Lithuanian immigrants, he grew up in deprived circumstances in London's East End and was obliged to leave school at 14 to work. Thanks to Birkbeck College, however, where the fees were modest and the standards high, he was able to continue his studies at night. During his years at Birkbeck's art department (1907-1911), he received a sound training, won several prizes and produced his earliest-known self-portrait, now at Tate Britain. This same rigorous training enabled him to win a place at the Slade School of Fine Art, University College, London, which he attended from 1911 to 1914. He was staying with his sister, Minnie, in Cape Town when war broke out

That put an end to Rosenberg's hopes of earning a living through painting or writing. In 1915 he enlisted in the British army. He was killed near Arras on April 1, 1918, in the great German offensive. His remains are unidentified to this day and his only real memorial is a gravestone in France recording his name and his profession, 'Artist and Poet'.

It is proposed that the statue will be in Torrington Square on the Birkbeck College campus. The proximity to the two great learning centres in Rosenberg's life, Birkbeck and the Slade, make this an even more fitting memorial to his genius.The statue will be only the fifth statue of a poet in London and only the second in Britain of a Jewish literary figure (the other being Benjamin Disraeli).

**Payments to: Jeecs-Rosenberg Statue appeal, c/o Clive Bettington,
P.O. Box 57317, London E1 3WG www.jeecs.org.uk/rosenberg**

THE DEVIL'S PORRIDGE

Daleside, Butterdales Road, Eastriggs, Annan, Dumfries and Galloway, DG12 6TU

Eastriggs and Gretna Heritage have launched a fundraising campaign to raise £50,000 for a statue and memorial to commemorate the contribution made by women in two world wars.

The statue of a munitions girl will be erected at the new Devil's Porridge Museum which is set to open in 2014, in time to commemorate the centenary of World War One.

The Devil's Porridge tells the amazing story of "the greatest factory on earth" where 30,000 women and men came from all over to produce cordite. 12,000 female workers mixed the volatile explosive by hand and did their bit to win the war and gain votes for women.

We are seeking small and large donations to be gift-aided to our cause. We are also seeking charitable trust support to make our project possible.

Please send donations made payable to Eastriggs and Gretna Heritage, (Scottish Charity No. SC031616.), c/o 2 Blake Terrace, Dornock Annan Dumfriesshire DG12 6SR

We welcome questions by e-mail to our Chairman Richard Brodie to: richardrbrod@aol.com

For more information about the Devil's Porridge museum, visit the website at
www.devilsporridge.co.uk

to remember
to honour
to study

THE GALLIPOLI ASSOCIATION

www.gallipoli-association.org

SONIA BIDWELL – TEXTILE ARTIST & STORYTELLER

Sonia is well known across Scotland for her unusual interpretations of myths and legends which she produces in wall hangings incoporating fabric, weaving and objets trouvés to make facinating works full of colour and hidden meaning.

Each year in her solo exhibitions she concentrates on a theme particular to that year's events. Her work has been seen at the Orkney Festival, the Edinburgh Scottish Story Telling Centre, The Highland Festival of Homecoming, the Highland Feis and regularly at smaller venues all over the Highlands.

This work originated from her time as a crofter on the Isle of Skye using wool from her own sheep to creat works of startling originality. Now retired, she has developed this into a unique body of work. In her role as a storyteller she is present at her exhibitions to explain the origins of her pieces and relate their tales.

Commissions and the staging of her own work to fit in with themed events are always welcome.

Sonia Bidwell – Abhras Studio, Lairg, Scotland. IV27 4EU
www.spanglefish.com/AbhrasStudio

ACKNOWLEDGEMENTS

Matt Jacobsen - OldMagazineArticles.com

Chris McCabe, Librarian, The Poetry Library, Southbank Centre, Belvedere Road, London

Rich Edwards of the Ella Wheeler Wilcox Society – www.ellawheelerwilcox.org

Theresa Saxon, Subject Co-ordinator, Literature and Cultures, School of Language, Literature and International Studies, University of Central Lancashire, Preston

Bairbre O'Hogan in Dublin for her help with biographical details of family friend Winifred Letts

Eurico Ventura Pereira & Maria de Lurdes Cruz Gomes of Coimbra, Portugal for informtion about Florbela Espanca and the Portuguese involvement in WW1

Kathrin Eckhart, Luxembourg

Will Kaufman, PhD, FRSA, FHEA - Professor of American Literature and Culture, University of Central Lancashire, Preston

Peter Parsley of Antwerp, Belgium for his help with the photo of Marie Nizet

Sonia Bridwell, Textile Artist/Storyteller – www.spanglefish

Seona Ford - Chair, Dorothy L Sayers Society - www.sayers.org.uk

Christen E. Runge - Assistant Curator, Art Collection, Special Collections Research Center, Lauinger Library, Georgetown University , USA

The Officers of The Gallipoli Association - http://www.gallipoli-association.org/

Clive Bettington of the Isaac Rosenberg Appeal, London – www.jeecs.org.uk

Dean Johnson of the Wilfred Owen Story, Argyle Street, Birkenhead, Wirral and author of "Bullets and Daffodils"

Janet Holmes of the Rathbone Studio, Argyle Street, Birkenhead, Wirral

Richard & Sheila of the Devil's Porridge Museum to the memory of the Munitions Workers. Gretna

Letters Page, The Times Newspaper, London - www.thetimes.co.uk

Dr. Ian Olson of Aberdeen

Dr. J. Whittredge and Professor G. Dawe, Trinity College, Dublin, Eire

Professor G. Williams of Bangor University, Wales

Professor Dr. Shaun Viljoen from Stellenbosch University, South Africa

The Riverside Writers Group from the Wirral Peninsular - http://riversidewriterswestkirby.blogspot.co.uk/p/anthology-2013.html

Jim Bennett of The Poetry Kit website - www.poetrykit.org

Elaine Edwards - who has helped me so much from Day One - from the Museum of Scotland in Edinburgh for her invaluable suggestions and continued support and encouragement.

Erica from the BHSOGS for her help and encouragement

Mrs K. Holyhead for showing me her Grandmother's wonderful notebook full of handwritten inspirational poems.

Mike Lyons for sending me a copy of his book about the Austrian Poet "Ingeborg Bachman enigma Selected Poems", Ariadne Press, 2011

Yoshihiko Makanishi from Japan for helping me to find a Japanese poet

Leslie Johnson, Wirral for her encouragement

Les Voix Perdues – A Capella singers from Belgium

Emma van Bijnen from Amsterdam

Stephen Cribari, a poet who teaches law at the University of Minnesota, America and the American Notre Dame Law School in London

Suzanne Raitt, Professor of English at the College of William and Mary, Williamsburg, Virginia, America

Rianne from Feetwood Library, Lancashire

Arnold Sumner of Arnold Antiques, St. Annes on the Sea, Lancashire

Lisette Matano of Georgetown University Library, Washington, USA

The Cross and Cockade Society

The Gallagher Family at Park's Art Deco Café, Stanley Park, Blackpool

Roger Phillips, BBC Radio Merseyside

Mrs J. Kingsland, Archivist at Downe House School, Berkshire

Sheena Gaskell and her Team at the Birkenhead Reference Library, Birkenhead, Wirral

Nelson Library, Lancashire

Roger Hull, Liverpool Records Office

Furry Tails, Wood Street, St. Annes

Soki Kotavo, Japan for his help in finding a poem in Japanese

Dean Echenberg of www.warpoetrycollection.com

Michael Halewood of the Antiquarian Bookshop in Friargate, Preston

Lt. Col. (Prof) G.E. Visser of the Department of Military History at Stellenbosch University, South Africa

The North Eueston Hotel, Fleetwood, Lancashire

And last but not least, my thanks to Paul for his endless patience, perseverance and encouragement – without him none of this would be possible.

BIBLIOGRAPHY - JULY 2013

BOOKS

AKHMATOVA, Anna: "Belaya Staya" (Petrograd: Hyperborea, 1917)

AKHMATOVA, Anna: "Anno Domini MCMXXI" (Petrograd, 1922)

BATES, Rachel: "Danae And Other Poems" (London: Erskine MacDonald Ltd, 1922)

BENSON, Stella: "Twenty" (London: Macmillan, 1918)

BRITTAN, Vera: "Testament Of Friendship: The Story Of Winifred Holtby" (London: Macmillan, 1940)

BILTON, David .- "Images of War The Germans in Flanders 1914" (Pen & Sword, Barnsley, 2012)

BIRN, Antony and BIRN, Nicholas. Eds.- "Voices from the Front Line' (Summersdale Publishers Ltd., Chichester, Sussex, 2008)

BOORMAN, Derek.- "A Century of Remembrance. 100 Outstanding British War Memorials". (Pen & Sword Books, Barnsley, Yorkshire, 2005)

CHRISTIE Mallowan, Agatha: "The Road of Dreams" (London: Geoffrey Bles, 1924)

CLARKE, G.H. Ed.- "A Treasury of War Poetry British and American Poems 1914 - 1919 (Hodder & Stoughton, London, 1917)

DELARUE-MARDRUS, Lucie: "Ferveur"(Paris : Editions De La Revue Blanche, 1902)

EDWARDS, Mabel C. and Booth, Mary, Editors; "The Fiery Cross: An Anthology". (London: Grant Richards Ltd,1915).

ESPANCA, Florbela: "Livro De Magoas" (Lisbon: Tipografia Mauricio, 1919)

FEIS, Agnita: "Oorloog. Verzen in Staccato" (Self Published, 1915)

FOWLER WRIGHT. S. (Ed.).- "Poets of Merseyside An Anthology of Present Day Poetry"(London: Merton Press Ltd,1923)

FOX SMITH, Cicely: "Fighting Men", (London: Elkin Matthews, 1916)

GARVIN, John William ed: "Canadian Poets" (Toronto: McClelleland, Goodchild & Stewart, 1916)

GOLDSTEIN, JOSHUA S.- "War and Gender: How Gender shapes the War System and Vice Versa" (Cambridge University Press, Cambridge, 2001)

GORE-JONES, Alice: "Troop Trains".(Adelaide: Hassell, 1917)

GUGLIELMINETTI, Amalia: "I Seduzioni"(Turin : Editori S Lattes & C Librai, 1909)

HIGGONET, Margaret, Ed. - "Lines of Fire - Women Writers of World War I" (London: Penguin Books, 1999)

HOLLIS, Matthew and KEEGAN, Paul Eds.- "101 Poems against War" (London: Faber and Faber, 2003)

124

HOLT, Tonie and Valmai and ZEEPVAT, Charlotte, Eds. – "Poets of the Great War" (Barnsley: Pen & Sword Books Ltd, 1999)

HOLTBY, Winifred, Webb, Antony (ed) – "Poems And Verse Of Winifred Holtby" (Newcastle Upon Tyne: Cambridge Scholars Publishing, 2012)

HOWELLS, William Dean ed: "King Albert's Book – a tribute to the Belgian king and people from representative men and women throughout the world" (New York: Hearst's International Library Co, 1914)

KHAN, Noshee, Ed.- "Women's Poetry of the First World War" (Lexington: University Press of Kentucky, 1988)

LARKIN, Philip.- "The Oxord Book of Twentieth Century Verse Chosen by Philip Larkin" (Oxford: Oxford University Press, 1973)

LASKER-SCHULER, Elsa: "Der Siebente Tag"(Berlin: Verlag des Vereins fur Kunst, Amelang-sche Buchhandung, 1905)

LASKER-SCHULER, Elsa: "Die Kuppel (Die Gedichte - Zweiter Teil)"(Berlin: Verlag Paul Cassirer, 1920)

LETTS, Winifred Mary: "Hallow-een And Poems Of The War" (New York: EP Dutton & Company, 1916).

LINECAR, Howard.- "Aerpolanes of World War 1"(London: Ernest Benn Ltd, 1967)

LLWYD, Alan, Ed. - "Out of the Fire of Hell. Welsh Experiences of the Great War 1914 – 1918 in prose and verse" (Ceredigion: Gomer Press, 2008)

MACDONALD, John with ZELIKO, Cimpric. - "Caporetto and the Isonzo Campaign The Italian Front 1915 – 1918" (Barnsley: Pen & Sword Military, 2011)

MARTIN, Stephen, Ed.- "Poems of the First World War" (London: Orion Publishing Group, 1993)

MERCIER-NIZET, Marie: "Pour Axel De Missie" (Brussels: Editions De La Vie Intellectuelle, 1923)

MICHAEL, Moina Belle & Roan, Leonard: "The Miracle Flower: The Story Of The Flanders Field Poppy" (Philadelphia: Dorrance & Co, 1941)

MISTRAL, Gabriela: "Desolacion - Poemas"; (New York: Instituto de las Espanas en Estados Unidos, 1922)

NAIDU, Sarojini: "The Golden Threshold" (London: William Heinemann, 1905)

NEGRI, Ada: "Esile" (Milan: Editori Fratelli Treves, 1914)

NOAKES, Vivien, Ed. - "Voices of Silence The Alternative Book of First World War Poetry" (Stroud: Sutton Publishing Ltd, 2006)

PAWLIKOWSKA, Maria Kossakow: "Niebieskie Migdały" (Krakow: Spolki Wydawniczej, 1922)

POLE, Stephen and WHEAL, Elizabeth-Anne Eds. - "Dictionary of the First World War" (Barnsley: Pen & Sword Military Classics, 2003)

REILLY, Catherine. Ed. - "Scars upon my Heart" (London: Virago Press, 1981)

SHOVE, Fredegond: "Dreams And Journeys" (Oxford: BH Blackwell, 1918)

SINCLAIR, May: "A Journal of Impressions in Belgium" (New York: Macmillan, 1915)

SITWELL, Edith et al: "Wheels – An Anthology Of Verse" (Oxford: BH Blackwell, 1916)

SITWELL Edith ed et al: "Wheels – Fourth Cycle" (Oxford: BH Blackwell, 1919)

SMITH, William James, Ed. – "Granger's Index to Poetry" (London: Columbia University Press, 1973)

SÖDERGRAN, Edith – "Dikter" (Borga / Porvoo: Holger Schildts Forlag, 1916)

SPIRIDONOVIC- SAVIC, Jelena: "Sa Uskih Staza" (Belgrade: Izdanje SB Cvijanovica, 1919)

SPIRIDONOVIC-SAVIC, Jelena: "Pergamente" (Belgrade: Izdanje SB Cvijanovica, 1923)

VACARESCO, Helene: "Le Jardin Passioné" (Paris: Plon-Nourrit et Cie, 1908)

WEBB, Mary: "Poems and The Spring Of Joy" by Mary Webb (London: Jonathan Cape,1928).

WHEELER WILCOX, Ella: "Poems Of Optimism" (London: Gay & Hancock, 1915)

WHITEHOUSE, Arch.- "The Zeppelin Fighters" (London: Robert Hale,1968)

XIN, Bing: "Infinite Stars" (China: 1921)

MAGAZINES

"The Art World" in January 1917, Volume 1, No. 4
"Neue Jugend" magazine, Vol 1 Issue 11/12, Feb/Mar 1917, Page 245

INTERNET SITES

http://oldpoetry.com/Madeline_Ida__Bedford__poems
http://www.firstworldwar.com/poetsandprose/sinclair.htm
http://www.greatwardifferent.com/Great_War/Nurses_6/Sinclair_01.htm
http://english.siu.edu/Resources/World%20War%20I%20Women%20Poets.pdf
http://members.home.nl/ja.goris/poetrywwl.htm
http://sophie.byu.edu/?q=node/3185
http://www.scuttlebuttsmallchow.com
http://www.firstworldwar.com/features/womenww1
http://fr.wikipedia.org/wiki/Lucie_Delarue-Mardrus
http://allpoetry.com/poem/8610927-_A_Fight_to_a_Finish_-by-S_Gertrude_Ford
http://www.whscms.org.uk/index.php?category_id=1994
The First World War Poetry Digital Archive, University of Oxford www.oucs.ox.ac.uk/www1lit

FACEBOOK GROUPS

WW1 Buffs
Wolrd War One Remembered
World War 1: Remembering the Great War
A Canadian Solier Memorial Site for our WW1 & WW2 Heroes
WAR MEMORIALS should be respected as a place to honour the fallen
The Rifles Living History Society
Vera Brittain
The Wilfred Owen Association
Ingleborough Road War Memorial Cause